Revising & Editing

Using Models and Checklists to Promote
Successful Writing Experiences

Les Parsons

Pembroke Publishers Limited

© **2001 Pembroke Publishers**
538 Hood Road
Markham, Ontario, Canada L3R 3K9
www.pembrokepublishers.com

Distributed in the U.S. by Stenhouse Publishers
477 Congress Street
Portland, ME 04101
www.stenhouse.com

We acknowledge the financial support of the Government of Canada through
the Book Publishing Industry Development Program (BPIDP) for our
publishing activities.

Canadian Cataloguing in Publication Data

Parsons, Les, 1943-
   Revising & editing: using models and checklists to promote successful
writing experiences

Includes index.
ISBN 1-55138-130-3

1. Creative writing (Middle school). 2. Creative writing (Secondary
education). 3. English language – Rhetoric – Study and teaching (Middle
school). 4. English language – Rhetoric – Study and teaching (Secondary).
5. Editing – Study and teaching (Middle school). 6. Editing – Study and
teaching (Secondary). I. Title. II. Title: Revising and editing.

LB1576.P367 2001   808'.042'0712   C00-932641-3

Editor: Kate Revington
Cover Design: John Zehethofer
Typesetting: JayTee Graphics

Printed and bound in Canada
9 8 7 6 5 4 3 2

Contents

Preface

Computers have not solved the problems of revising and editing in the classroom. Every advantage arising out of word-processing programs has been matched by a contrary disadvantage. As teachers at all grade levels will attest, students still don't understand revision and their idea of editing often begins and ends with spell check. More than ever, teachers need to address the direct teaching of specific revising and editing skills. This book offers concrete and effective ways to meet that challenge.

Experts have long espoused the benefits of modelling writing behaviors; unfortunately, since most teachers aren't professional writers, they hardly know where to begin. At the core of this book, however, are eight modelling series that consist of student writing samples, peer-revision comments, and illustrations and assignments that allow students to vicariously experience successful revision. The series also provide detailed instructions to direct the teacher in guiding students. As well as models, teachers will find a wealth of guidelines, checklists, and background material to support their teaching. Models and checklists are formatted for photocopying or for use on an overhead projector. This book is truly a toolkit for the teaching of revising and editing skills.

CHAPTER 1

Drafting in the Computer Age

The Impact of the Computer on Student Writing

Desktop publishing has revolutionized the writing process in schools.
At the outset, word processing eliminated the need for mindless recopying and the myriad problems associated with handwriting. The days of laboriously transcribing by hand, rough copy after rough copy, until some semblance of a respectable finished version is achieved are gone forever. Since text can be manipulated so quickly and efficiently, revising can also be swift and effortless. Spell-check and grammar-check programs buttress the editing process. Multiple formatting features and sophisticated graphics capabilities can enhance and enliven the appearance of the text, while laser printing delivers instant and near-perfect hard copies. Even the stumbling blocks that used to be cited as schools implemented computers into their curricula have dropped away one by one.

With the worldwide spread of affordable home computers, high-speed access to the Internet, a wide range of educational CDs available to parents, and the allure of sophisticated gaming modules, many children come to school with confident keyboarding skills and a ready familiarity with the technology. Teachers who once mourned the death of letter writing are now discovering more and more of their students routinely conversing by e-mail and surfing the Web. The current generation of computers, moreover, allows the integration of systems at home and school, regardless of platform; students intrinsically understand the portability of their work stations, routinely transferring tasks from home to school and back again. With word processing and the writing process, the medium, indeed, has become the message — or so it would seem.

In reality, composing on the computer has been a mixed blessing. Like the flip side of a coin, each advantage offered by the computer comes complete with a problematic side.

The pristine, print-ready text on the screen, for example, enhanced with formatting features, such as specialized fonts or title highlighting, looks *too* perfect. Regardless of the quality of the content or the correctness of the language, many students become mesmerized by the appearance of the page. With the flawless "product" in full view on the monitor and a hard copy only a simple printing command away, personal reflection and significant, meaningful revision are neglected for the ease of superficial, mechanical editing.

Many students are dependent on the editing programs to ferret out errors and are often oblivious to the limitations of these programs. They, in effect, transfer responsibility for their own use of language to the computer. "But I used spell check" becomes the first line of defence in response to any criticism of the text.

Meanwhile, the instantaneous and informal nature of e-mail communication has blurred the lines between spoken and written language. In the quest for speed, e-mail language assumes the characteristics of vanity licence plates, as students ask, "How RU 2day?"

For all these reasons, and despite the power and ease of word processing, chances are good that a student writing on a computer will wind up with a fabulous-looking, but inferior piece of writing and not know where to start to make it any better. In the computer age, the need to teach revision and editing skills endures.

You Say "Editing"; I Say "Revising"

Consider these two important questions:

> What's the difference between revising and editing?
> Which comes first or can they both be done together?

The answers to these questions are crucial to the development of an effective writing program at any level. The more confused students are about the concepts embedded in these questions, the more trouble they have applying and internalizing effective revising/editing strategies.

In theory, the drafting process should be simple to understand and to implement. The key to good writing is having something worthwhile to say. Clear thinking helps the writer get the message across effectively, and revision is the heart of the thinking process.

The content of the writing must be dealt with first. Through the revision process, the content is manipulated and altered in a number of specific ways to ensure that the meaning encapsulated in the writing will be effectively presented to the reader. Whether students use the computer or not, their task is to filter through the content, discarding, recycling, changing, rearranging, and recreating.

The clarity of presentation is also affected by the degree to which mechanical aspects of the language, such as punctuation, spelling, sentence and paragraph structure, and usage, are congruent with standard practice. That part of the drafting process is called editing.

In spite of decades of writing process or writer's workshop programs, however, a great many students and a large number of teachers still remain confused about the difference between editing and revising. It doesn't help, of course, that the words "revise" and "edit" are often used interchangeably in reference texts. For example, here are two excerpts from *Webster's New World Dictionary*:

> **edit**: To **revise** and make ready a manuscript for publication

> **revise**: to read over carefully and correct, improve or update where necessary

Confusing the two processes is only part of the story. Since revising and editing are two separate processes, they must be *conducted* separately to preserve the integrity and effectiveness of the drafting process itself.

The demands of the two tasks and the way they're valued lie at the heart of the real problem with drafting. Editing is a relatively straightforward undertaking: Look for errors and correct them. Although students detect a few usage and punctuation errors, they tend to focus on correct spelling in their approach to editing. In their spelling programs and in the way teachers routinely correct and deduct marks from their written work for spelling, students learn the importance placed on the word and on correct spelling. When revising, they focus on word substitution; when editing, they primarily look for spelling errors. Both tasks require comparatively low-level thinking skills.

This focus on words means that most higher-level revision techniques are usually neglected. These techniques require reflection and review, calling upon students to substitute, add, delete, and reorder words, phrases, sentences, ideas, and even entire sections of a draft. Since the process is so difficult, how much revision is actually occurring in classrooms?

A Revision Report Card

How do your students stack up when applying revision techniques? Do the following survey. Keep one of your classes in mind and complete the survey for the kinds of revision activities you witness as they work through their drafting process. A critique of student revision practices follows the survey.

Diagnostic Survey on Class Revision Practices

How often do your students engage in the following revision activities?

	Always	Often	Sometimes	Rarely	Never
1. Substitute words?	A	O	S	R	N
2. Add or delete words?	A	O	S	R	N
3. Reorder words?	A	O	S	R	N
4. Substitute phrases?	A	O	S	R	N
5. Add or delete phrases?	A	O	S	R	N
6. Reorder phrases?	A	O	S	R	N
7. Substitute sentences?	A	O	S	R	N
8. Add or delete sentences?	A	O	S	R	N
9. Reorder sentences?	A	O	S	R	N
10. Substitute ideas?	A	O	S	R	N
11. Add or delete ideas?	A	O	S	R	N
12. Reorder ideas?	A	O	S	R	N
13. Substitute sections?	A	O	S	R	N
14. Add or delete sections?	A	O	S	R	N
15. Reorder sections?	A	O	S	R	N

Not all revision activities are equal. The easiest and most frequently attempted revision activity is substitution; the most difficult and rarely attempted activity is reordering. The easiest and most frequently chosen focus for any of these activities is a word; the most difficult and rarely attempted focus is an idea. With this hierarchy in mind, what patterns did you detect in your class's approach to revision? How well do they compare with the following critique of students in general and at the primary, junior, intermediate, and secondary levels?

At all levels, students revise their written work reluctantly and in a relatively narrow and limited manner. The working conception of revision is usually word substitution; in effect, using synonyms either to avoid repetition or to substitute a "better" word. When revising, students generally prefer to substitute; they add or delete less frequently and they rarely reorder. The measured, incremental development from grade to grade in revision skills, moreover, is a myth. Granted, intermediate students, in general, make a huge leap in their ability to revise their writing and that level remains more or less constant throughout secondary school. The determining factor, here, is developmental.

After puberty, when adolescents are able to metacognate, that is, to think about thinking, they bring a whole new perspective to why and how they write. With a more mature cognitive and emotional matrix in place, they can truly begin to see through another's eyes and understand the function of writing as a life skill. They begin to understand that people write to make sense of and to help cope with their world (and ultimately themselves).

Even so, and in spite of the relative growth from their elementary years, intermediate students still possess only minimal revising skills. The most common revision activities remain the addition, deletion, or substitution of words. Instances of adding, deleting, or substituting phrases are less frequent; adding, deleting, or substituting sentences is less frequent still; and adding, deleting, and substituting ideas in or sections of a piece of writing are almost non-existent. The reordering of words, phrases, sentences, ideas, or sections is seldom attempted at any level.

Clearly, students at all levels have difficulty with the whole notion of revising. Curriculum guidelines just as clearly require that students learn how to revise. Before looking at solutions to the problem, let's probe a little more deeply why students have so much difficulty with revision.

The Culture of Editing

A sea change occurs in how children regard learning as they pass through the grades, and that change critically affects how students come to view revising.

Young people in the primary grades, for example, explore their world in a hands-on, egocentric, and unreflective manner. As they explore, change is a constant. Their understanding of the properties and qualities of their world shifts and changes from moment to moment and in a recursive manner. That round peg didn't fit into that square hole yesterday, but it might today. Besides, maybe a different round peg will fit better. Adults consult norms to establish objective truth; deviation from the norm is a mistake. Children consult experience to establish subjective truth; deviation from the norm is an adventure. Mistakes are foreign to their approach to learning. That's why they love the spontaneity of crafts and the impermanence of sand and water play.

They also role-play naturally and freely, allowing dialogue and narrative to shift and change from moment to moment, from day to day. Beginning readers will hold a storybook and flip the pages as they tell an invented story that has little relation to the actual content. Their personal narrative, however, is always pregnant with personal meaning. In a child's idiosyncratic world, the focus is on the *I*.

Whatever they're doing, children always know what they mean or mean to represent. That's why their paintings remain first drafts and, since the children can describe each representation in detail, perfectly composed from their point of view. Besides, a painting is simply a jumping off point into their personal narratives, just as a puppet play might be, or an encounter in sand. Not surprisingly, as Lewis Carroll reflects in *Through the Looking-Glass*, when they begin to write, children write from the same perspective.

> "When *I* use a word," Humpty Dumpty said, in rather a scornful tone, "it means just what I choose it to mean — neither more nor less."
>
> "The question is," said Alice, "whether you *can* make words mean so many different things."
>
> "The question is," said Humpty Dumpty, "which is to be the master — that's all."

Young children are the masters of their own language. Since they always know what they want words to mean, they feel comfortable using invented spellings, idiosyncratic punctuation, and truncated sentences. As with their first-draft paintings, their written words are starting points in their expression, rather than end-points. The story behind a particular painting will change from day to day. Young children feel free to elaborate at will and imbue the initial creation with added layers of personal experience and meaning. As with their paintings, whatever is written down never restricts the ever-changing kaleidoscope of images in their heads. Since whatever they mean to say is ever-changing, their original "written-down" expression, by definition, remains rooted in the past and subject to change. The concept of a final version, in this context, is nonsensical.

Even when they begin to read, children cleave to the primacy of personal meaning, much to the chagrin of parents and teachers. Adults are disconcerted when, in their oral reading, children say "home" instead of "house" or "The cat jumped up on the table" for "The cat leaped onto the table." Since children are the masters of their own language, words follow meaning. For adults, on the other hand, words are the master; meaning follows the word. Any deviation is dissonant. Both in reading and in writing, standardization is the goal.

The inexorable push to standardization results in a narrow and prescriptive understanding of what good writing is all about. Since adults accept the content of their writing wholeheartedly and seem to quibble only about the form that it takes, children intrinsically learn what they need to attend to once they get down what they want to say. To many children, the rule seems to be to make sure that everything is spelled correctly. In this way, children learn that the function of their reading and writing is subject to its form. They learn to limit their reading only to the specific words on the page. Anything else is a mistake. They also learn that the meaning of their writing, as well, is limited to the specific words on the page and that those words must conform to standard, acceptable patterns. Anything else is a mistake. Written expression under these conditions necessarily becomes an anomaly, an adult construct in a child's world. *deviation from the rule.*

A child's inclination to spontaneity and immediacy is suppressed to conform to an adult's perception of standardization through editing. Unfortunately, that view of written language indelibly colors how children approach written expression from that point on. Is it any wonder that so many students of all ages obsess about editing the surface features of their written work and seem oblivious to the need to revise?

Teachers from the junior grades on, of course, attempt to get their students back on the right track. In writing process or writer's workshop classes, students are instructed in a new set of priorities: content before form, meaning before surface features, revising before editing. In the context of what's actually happening in classrooms, however, that message often becomes, "Believe what we say, not what we do."

From a student's standpoint, content before form is an interesting notion; but, in the real world, getting the form right is worth marks. In the content areas, teachers routinely subtract marks on tests and essays for spelling and usage errors. Even in language programs, students are rewarded for letter-perfect spelling and penalized for mistakes. Imperfections in usage are red-lined and sent back for correction before the content is ever evaluated. Granted, teachers have pressures, expectations, and priorities of their own to deal with. No one's to blame. But, by first understanding why students are so resistant to the concept of revision, we can then develop strategies that will improve their revision techniques.

Teaching the Drafting Process

Revision can be taught as concretely and as productively as editing. In Chapter 4, for example, a series of models are offered to help teachers demonstrate and articulate what writers think about, say, and do when they're revising. Teachers and teaching are central to improving student revision. For students to become more competent in the full drafting process, teachers need to assume a variety of roles in the classroom writing dynamic.

As *mentors*, teachers demonstrate or model the process of meaningful drafting. They present writing as a multifaceted, open-ended activity in which adults and students take part for a variety of reasons and in a variety of ways across the curriculum. In that same role, they maintain a continuing dialogue with the younger writers, supporting, advising, and guiding as directed by their students' needs. (Please see specific models for teacher demonstrations in Chapter 4.)

As *supervisors*, teachers design an evaluation system that will support the implementation of specific drafting strategies and reinforce specific drafting expectations. In this supervisory role, teachers display respect for each individual's personal mode of expression, monitor how their students are functioning as writers, discover ways to diagnose their needs, and help them develop solutions to their drafting problems.

As *editors*, teachers establish and communicate an objective, knowledgeable, and experienced perspective. Their counsel helps student writers evaluate the effectiveness of their own pieces of writing and make the crucial decisions about pursuing further revision and publishing/marking or discontinuing the cycle and starting on another project.

As far as revising and editing are concerned, teacher expectations will depend on the level at which individual students are functioning and the type of intervention required to move them with success from that level. A reluctant, insecure, and immature writer and a proficient, confident, and sophisticated writer bring far different skills, attitudes, and experiences to the demands of drafting. Both need to experience success and both need to improve their skills. Given their different starting points, some program modification and a different emphasis in expectations are essential to their development as writers.

Three representative profiles of student writers follow: emerging dependent, transitional independent, and maturing interdependent. As with any attempt to classify levels of competence, these general stages have been chosen for the sake of convenience alone. Isolating stages, however, affords an opportunity to discuss how best to facilitate the needs of student writers with different sets of skills. Along the continuum of writing proficiencies, the three categories should be visualized as overlapping and inclusive stages of a non-linear and recursive process. Writing at any one level may indeed exhibit some of the characteristics of either or both of the other two levels. Given these limitations, the competency levels attempt to describe stages of skill and confidence, regardless of grade level. The categories also do not in any way conform to the manner in which teachers customarily grade writing samples for summative purposes. In terms of conventional evaluative labels, a writing sample from any of the categories, such as emerging dependent, might be marked A, B, C, or D, depending on the standards of the specific grade level.

For each of the three stages, the writer profile is followed by an initial suggested plan for program modification and possible teacher expectations for both revising and editing.

Emerging dependent stage

WRITER PROFILE

- The writer wants teacher to direct topic, genre, and length; often unsure how to start; becomes easily "stalled."
- He or she may have a similar, mechanistic approach to reading.
- Writing is usually simply and briefly phrased; follows patterns of spoken language.
- Descriptive language is used sporadically and by rote.
- The writer is overly concerned with mechanical correctness, especially spelling; sticks to tried and secure vocabulary.
- Conventional usage is haphazardly and inconsistently applied.
- The student is fixated on editing and has little understanding of revision.

PROGRAM MODIFICATIONS

- Enable reading with individualized materials.
- Encourage pre-writing brainstorming alone and with peers.
- Encourage frequent peer-revision conferences.

- Enable word processing and emphasize benefits of spell check.
- Model the routines of peer conferences.

- Encourage substituting, adding, and deleting of words.
- Expect beginning of substituting, adding, and deleting of phrases.
- Expect positive functioning in peer conferences.
- Expect computer spell check for editing.

Transitional independent stage

WRITER PROFILE

- Student writes spontaneously and with enthusiasm from real and vicarious experiences.
- Writing is often influenced by genre and style of favorite reading materials.
- Writing is often extended, obviously crafted, and marked by a variety of sentence structures.
- The writer consciously and purposefully employs descriptive language; use of metaphor is developing.
- The writer is more concerned with own ideas and inventions than with mechanical correctness and takes risks with vocabulary; as a consequence, mechanical errors may be frequent.
- Conventional usage is generally understood and applied.
- The writer is attracted to peer-revision strategies, but may be impatient with the full editing cycle, including proofreading.

PROGRAM MODIFICATIONS

- Enable maximum writing time in class.
- Model reordering of words, phrases, and sentences to facilitate drafting.
- Encourage multiple peer-editing conferences.

DRAFTING EXPECTATIONS

- Expect continued substituting, adding, and deleting of words, phrases, and sentences.
- Expect beginning of reordering of words, phrases, and sentences.
- Expect effective use of peer-editing conferences.

Maturing interdependent stage

WRITER PROFILE

- The student self-selects purpose, genre, and length of writing.
- The writer is usually an independent, insightful, fluent reader.
- He or she often employs sophisticated, stylistic features from reading in own writing.

- Writing is extended, crafted, and marked by a variety of complex sentence structures.
- Use of descriptive language and metaphor is refined.
- The writer has an assured understanding of conventional usage.
- The student writes independently, but is attracted to the collaborative features of a writer's workshop approach.
- The writer uses peer-revision and peer-editing strategies to the fullest extent.

PROGRAM MODIFICATIONS

- Enable maximum writing independence.
- Model the substituting, adding, deleting, and reordering of sections and ideas.

DRAFTING EXPECTATIONS

- Expect continued substituting, adding, deleting, and reordering of words, phrases, and sentences.
- Expect beginning of substituting, adding, deleting, and reordering of sections and ideas.
- Expect material handed in for marking to be "camera ready."

The Use of Writing Folders in the Drafting Process

Writing folders are an integral part of any kind of programming, teaching, and remediation in revising and editing. They facilitate the drafting process and preserve the results of that process over time. The physical structure of such portfolios varies widely and is important only to the extent that it supports and mirrors the writing process and supplies valid evidence of growth in written fluency. Whether a student uses a file folder, a loose-leaf binder, or a notebook, that "folder" should mirror and facilitate the writing process.

For a number of reasons, a usable writing folder is essential if the writing process is to flourish in classrooms. Students and teachers alike need that "mirror" to help them reflect on and learn from specific, individual writing patterns over time. Students need the organizational and record-keeping assistance, as well as the freedom to pursue a recursive, ever-changing investigation into meaning, that a folder can offer. Teachers want a folder to stimulate the kinds of activities they perceive as beneficial to young writers and they also need the objective evidence a folder contains to make summative decisions. *additive/cummulative*

The principal benefit of a writing folder is in opening up an effective and efficient process. Use of a folder encourages exploratory writing (rough drafts) in a variety of genres. It permits revisions of selected pieces, whereby students incorporate peer/adult response; shape and rework material; and offer assistance to others. It also promotes the editing (the proofreading process) of selected pieces for which students consult reference material, such as dictionaries, thesauri, and usage handbooks; apply peer-editing strategies; focus on punctuation, spelling, sentence and paragraph structure and usage; and present a final, print-ready version. The process culminates in the marking/publishing of selected pieces in a variety of genres.

Should Writing Be a Computer-Driven Process?

Has keyboarding made handwriting obsolete? At what point in a contemporary writing program, if at all, should student writers shut down their computers and turn on their pencils?

While the behavior of professional writers should never direct classroom practice, adult idiosyncrasies, in this regard, can be instructive. (William F. Buckley, Jr., and Robert B. Parker, for example, are two professional authors who seldom revise; their first drafts are their last drafts.) Some authors claim that the connection between the hand and the brain is hard-wired for thought, that the flexibility and stuttering, non-linear reactions of a pen or pencil mirror the nature of the mind recursively searching for meaning. Other authors never see a hard copy of their writing until the printer churns out the final draft. Some writers use the computer for prose, but handwrite poetry; others switch to handwriting only when creating dialogue. The variations go on and on. Whether different and innate qualities imbue keyboarding and handwriting or professional writers attach those qualities to them, however, seems beside the point. Adult authors use whatever means at their disposal to formulate and process meaning. If the medium is the message, they choose the medium that best serves their personal visions. They aren't bound by inflexible rules.

If adult authors are all over the map in their relationship to and use of computers, so are classroom teachers. Some teachers have embraced the technology to such an extent that student writing can be conceived, revised, edited, and even evaluated before ever being printed; at the other extreme, some teachers insist that students handwrite their initial drafts, transcribing only the final version at the computer. The solutions teachers have devised to reconcile their own beliefs about learning in general and the nature of writing specifically with the burgeoning computer technology span these extremes and all combinations in between.

Compounding the issue is the complexity of the writing process itself and the individual needs of each developing student writer. Merely to state that writing is recursive and individualistic doesn't begin to sketch how haphazard, egocentric, and just plain messy the process looks to an outsider or how difficult it is to fit into the regulated, public, and standardized world of the school. How teachers resolve the issue of a handwritten or computer-driven process can have a profound impact on how individual writers mature and develop.

Handwriting versus keyboarding

If students have access to word-processing programs and choose to use them, they should be supported in that regard for the following reasons:

- Some of your students have sophisticated keyboarding skills; the frustration they would experience in handwriting an essay would be analogous to printing the material with a primary crayon.
- The computer is tailor-made for manipulating and editing text.
- Copying by hand is a mind-numbing task; in the process of handwriting an edited draft, new errors inevitably emerge.

- Some students have such poor small-motor skills that handwriting is a laborious, daunting, and repellent prospect.
- At the end of the writing process lies evaluation; computer-generated material looks better, has fewer surface errors, and will probably get better marks than handwritten material.
- First-draft writing is a free-flowing, get-the-ideas-down kind of activity. Unless the writer finds handwriting personally more empowering or liberating or significantly faster, the writing might as well be done on the computer.

Nevertheless, focusing on a hard, or paper, copy is recommended in the following cases:

- During revision, writers find it difficult to get a clear holistic sense of the piece when viewing it one-half or one page at a time. When applying many of the higher-level revision skills, such as reordering sections or ideas, a case can be made for insisting on hard copies with three or four pages arranged side by side. Once the additions, deletions, substitutions, and reordering have been indicated by hand, the changes can be quickly and easily made at the keyboard.
- Since editing functions, such as spell check, are an integral component of word-processing programs, use the technology. Afterwards, augment that beginning stage with a more comprehensive look at a hard copy. Editing symbols (please see Chapter 5) can expedite the note making as the writers and their conference partners scour the material for the host of errors not addressed by the computer.

While the revision process precedes the editing process, *persistent* some overlap is understandable. Just like scratching a mosquito bite, inveterate computer users automatically and compulsively spell-check every page of writing they do, even first-draft material. If students do spell-check before revising, no harm is done as long as they then focus on revision tasks.

Revision and Risk Taking

The allurement of the perfect-looking page is hard to dispel. (See "The Perfect Page?: A Checklist for Students" on page 18.) Looking good is half the battle when the goal is an error-free piece of writing. While teachers talk about the value of learning from mistakes, students soon learn to make as few as possible. After all, a red pencil mark is a red pencil mark is a red pencil mark. While teachers, on one hand, encourage students to see the intrinsic value of writing as a way of understanding and coping with their world and their lives, students, on the other hand, see teachers, each and every day, evaluating every word they put down on paper. The more a student becomes focused on writing for marks, the more that student becomes tentative, unsettled, and vulnerable when faced with the act of writing. Some student writers reduce the chances for error further by restricting their expression to a small, but secure reservoir of tried and true, endlessly recycled language and themes.

The Perfect Page?
A Checklist for Students

When you laser-print your writing from a word-processing program, it looks terrific. In fact, the pages may appear perfect. That dazzling appearance, however, can be deceiving. Put the final draft of your next piece of writing to the following test. Look past the polished surface features and discover whether you've said what you've wanted to say in the way you wanted to say it. The points you can't check off in the affirmative should prompt you to do some further revising or editing.

- I've said what I wanted to say with this piece of writing. I've left nothing out. ☐

- I can point to a number of features I like about this writing. ☐

- I don't find any thoughts confusing, unfinished, or awkwardly worded. ☐

- I've read the first sentence of each paragraph and the thoughts flow in a way that makes sense. ☐

- I haven't repeated myself in the ideas, words, or expressions I've used. ☐

- If I wasn't sure of a word's meaning, I asked someone or looked it up. ☐

- The ending finishes the piece off in a satisfying way. ☐

- I've had someone else read my piece aloud to me and it sounds the way it should. ☐

- I've discussed the writing with someone else who has read it and that person feels the same way as I do about it. ☐

- I put the writing aside for a couple of days and then reread it. I still think it's great! ☐

In the topsy-turvy world of writing in school, students understandably have difficulty distinguishing between substance and surface. When students *do* concentrate on substance, revision requires even more risk taking. In the complex process of learning, affective and cognitive behaviors are two sides to the same coin. Approached strictly as an intellectual exercise, revising is a fascinating, problem-solving activity. Some professional writers, such as Katherine Paterson, revel in the challenge of the revision process, reluctantly passing on a manuscript to an editor only after countless drafts. Most student writers, however, lack the emotional maturity and security to wholeheartedly embrace a process that requires them to question the quality and delivery of their thoughts. Such objectivity is difficult for adults to achieve, let alone young people who are struggling to gain a sense of their own self-worth in so many personal ways. While student writers certainly need to be shown how to revise material effectively, they also need to be convinced that the rewards of revising are worth the risks. As outlined in the following chapter, collaboration has a key role to play in broadening a student's awareness of and approach to the revision process.

CHAPTER 2

Collaboration and the Drafting Process

An Overview

In schools, writing to learn and learning to write have vital collaborative components. In fact, collaboration occurs at all stages of the writing process. In pre-writing conferences, for example, conference partners brainstorm ideas, topics, scenarios, and questions. They also discuss related reading, current issues, and personal interests to further stimulate and enrich the context for writing.

After completing an initial draft, student authors have the option of engaging in peer-revision conferences to gauge the impact of the material on a reader and to guide decisions on how best to shape the material. The student authors, however, need to remain autonomous throughout the collaborative process. They can direct the conferences and reflect on their outcomes by keeping the following questions in mind:

- What have I asked the reader to do?
- What impact did my material have?
- How does this reaction compare with the impact I intended?
- What will I have to take out, put in, change, or rearrange?
- How can the reader help me further?
- What more do I want to know about my material?

At the same time, the readers must be prepared to accept direction from the writers and to offer constructive reactions to and suggestions about the material. The following questions serve to guide a reader's responses:

- What, specifically, has the writer asked me to help with?
- How did I respond personally to the material?
- What was I thinking about as I read?
- What aspects intrigued or attracted me?
- What, if anything, was confusing?

- What ideas or events were unclear?
- What, if anything, was left out or seemed out of place?
- How did I respond to the opening and closing, to the development of ideas, or to the pace?
- What people or events did I want to know more about?

When student writers are satisfied with the content of their material and have self-edited to the best of their abilities, they have the further option of enlisting the help of others in editing/proofreading conferences. The writer and reader together develop a final, print-ready draft by considering aspects of punctuation, spelling, sentence and paragraph structure, and usage. Chapters 3 and 4 offer specifics on peer conferences.

Dial C for Assistance

Classroom teachers face the task of accommodating student writers at both ends of the collaboration spectrum and at all stages in between. Mature, independent writers understand the value of collaboration in the writing process and know when they need help and what kind of help they need. Emerging, dependent writers, on the other hand, lack both the necessary confidence and experience to freely pursue outside intervention. Many reluctant writers, in fact, prefer to conceal their writing from everyone, including the teacher, as long as possible.

Teachers should build a certain amount of collaboration into their writing programs to support and instruct all students, but keep those requirements flexible enough to encourage and allow the growth of an individual writer's independence. Ideally, the student writer controls both the writing process itself and the degree of collaboration. (Please see the accompanying diagram, "Collaboration and the Writing Process.")

Peer and adult conferences comprise part of a writer's palette of tools, ready to be applied when required. As with telephone helplines, the writer initiates contact and directs both the content and the duration of the call. Peer and adult conferences are available at all stages of the writing process and can be conducted whenever and as often as the student writer deems necessary.

Although flexibility is important, teachers should also insist on a minimal amount of collaboration. While student writers can still determine when they need to call for a conference, for example, they should realize that at least one revision conference and one editing conference must be conducted before a piece of writing will be accepted for evaluation and/or publication. Naturally, if the material handed in would benefit from further revision or editing, the teacher can return it to the writer and stipulate what kind and how many additional conferences should be held.

Collaboration does work; students need to see that it does. As they become accustomed to peer and adult conferences, develop the confidence to initiate collaboration as needed, and see their writing improve, they will begin to freely exercise their options within the drafting process.

Collaboration and the Writing Process

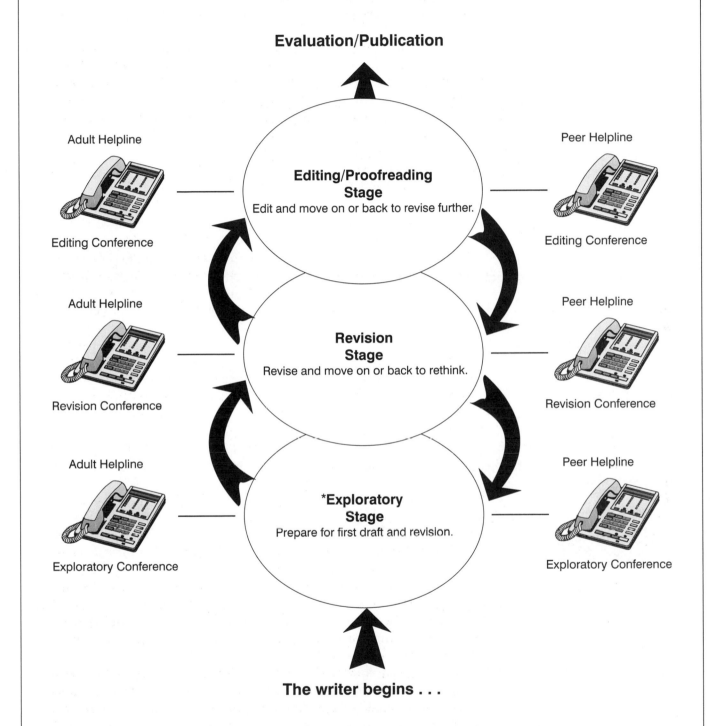

Evaluation/Publication

Adult Helpline

Editing Conference

Peer Helpline

Editing Conference

Editing/Proofreading Stage
Edit and move on or back to revise further.

Adult Helpline

Revision Conference

Peer Helpline

Revision Conference

Revision Stage
Revise and move on or back to rethink.

Adult Helpline

Exploratory Conference

Peer Helpline

Exploratory Conference

***Exploratory Stage**
Prepare for first draft and revision.

The writer begins . . .

*The Exploratory Stage may include brainstorming, reading, viewing, making notes, observing, representing, discussing, organizing information, planning, questioning, experimenting, researching, recording personal experiences, listening, reflecting, and listing.

Benefits of Peer-revision and Peer-editing Conferences

Peer-revision and peer-editing partners and small groups are specific applications of co-operative learning. The most powerful learning/teaching technique yet devised, co-operative learning is effective with all age groups and has consistently produced these benefits:

- improved learning results, especially for average students and students "at risk"
- higher academic achievement
- more effective problem solving
- increased higher-level thinking skills
- more positive attitudes towards subject
- greater motivation to learn

Peer-revision and peer-editing conferences offer additional benefits to the drafting process:

- Student authors gain a variety of perspectives on each draft.
- Peer exchanges are more extended and student language is more elaborate than in large-group, student-teacher interchanges.
- Conferences provide opportunities to build on each other's ideas, strengths, experience, and knowledge.
- Opinions and suggestions are voiced more freely.
- Criticism and suggestions are received more easily from a peer.
- Students develop a sense of responsibility for and ownership of the drafting process.
- Students interact in their own informal, spontaneous language.
- Students develop communication skills as they talk and learn with peers.
- Students develop self-confidence and feelings of self-worth.
- Conferences allows teachers to manage multi-level classes more effectively.

With all these advantages, the question is not whether to use peer-revision and peer-editing conferences, but rather how best to teach and implement the discussion techniques.

Teaching Peer-conference Skills

Partnerships for peer-revision and peer-editing conferences can be selected by the teacher, randomly, or by the participants themselves.

When teachers choose who works with whom, they usually do so for two reasons. Sometimes, they are attempting to redress some kind of perceived imbalance, such as exclusionary same-gender partnerships or constant equivalent-ability groupings. At other times, they are trying to correct potentially counterproductive situations, such as long-standing friendships interfering with group process or ESL students needing the stimulation of first-language users.

Hard and fast rules, however, should be avoided. For some students initially working with a friend or someone of similar ability may inject a needed sense of security and trust and encourage risk taking. On the other hand, some teachers worry about placing students of differing ability together, concerned that the more highly functioning student gains little from the partnership. The opposite is actually the case. In any mentoring situation, the mentor benefits most.

Clearly, teachers need to make their decisions about pairings based on their students' individual needs, abilities, and personalities. Some teachers begin the year by selecting all peer partners themselves and, as individuals learn more about each other and grow comfortable in a variety of pairings, gradually introduce student self-selection. Other teachers begin with random pairings or student self-selection and intercede only as circumstances warrant. Whatever the approach, teachers should ensure that students experience a variety of conference partners and that they receive instruction in how to operate responsibly and effectively in such small-group, discussion situations.

Successful collaboration in peer conferences doesn't just happen: students learn how to interact with others through positive coaching, practice, and reflection. Students must first learn about the skills they need to develop to work productively and purposefully in paired groupings. Regardless of the age or abilities of the students, the subject-specific area in which they're working, or the nature or content of the discussions, the set of skills remains the same.

These skills can be identified, taught, and, with practice and reflection, improved. The checklist "Questions That Promote Peer-conference Skills" isolates and highlights specific ways in which students can contribute to a successful peer conference. Students should never apply all these questions at any one time to a specific peer conference. Instead, the checklist introduces students to the self-reflection questions that help them identify and set personal interactive goals.

To develop their peer-conference skills, students need to become aware of the specific skills they need to refine, have frequent opportunities to practise them, and reflect regularly on how well they are applying them. Response journals, for example, offer an ideal way for students to comment on their own progress in developing these skills. A word of caution: Co-operative pairs operate best on a foundation of trust and respect. Never allow students in their journals to "inform" on what other students said or how they behaved. Instead, ask the students to reflect on and analyze their own behaviors during discussions, the strengths they usually display, as well as the skills they need to improve. After a peer conference, students might record in their journals the two or three skills they chose to focus on that day, how well they succeeded in applying them, or why they didn't, and what they intend to do in future to enhance their performance. Compare each student's observations with your own perceptions and address any discrepancies.

Over time, the response journal will present you with a profile of each student's involvement in peer conferences, the degree to which a student is developing mature self-awareness, the personal goals each student sets, and the kind of success a student is finding in the peer-conference process. This kind of written reflection, however, can easily become perfunctory and stultifying. Students may need to reflect in their journals on this issue only once a week. Teachers can then maintain freshness in the reflective process by introducing other techniques to encourage self-reflection and self-evaluation.

Questions That Promote Peer-conference Skills

The following questions highlight particular skills that will help you become an effective and responsible peer-conference partner. Before a peer conference, review the questions and choose two or three you intend to apply in that conference. After the conference, reflect on how well you succeeded.

During peer conferences, how frequently and successfully do you

• express appreciation for specific, positive aspects of the writing?

• make the writer feel worthwhile, even though you may be critical of parts of the writing?

• suggest alternate ideas or expressions in areas in which you are critical?

• offer facts and reasons to support your opinions?

• listen carefully so that you can ask clarifying questions or offer clarifying statements?

• reply freely to the writer's questions, problems, and concerns?

• share equally in the talking without dominating the discussion?

• go out of your way to help the other person have his or her turn to speak?

• speak up without cutting off the other person or shortchanging discussion of a particular issue?

• indicate in your gestures, facial expressions, or posture that you're interested in what is being said?

• indicate whether or not you agree with the ideas or decisions of the writer and why you do or don't?

• consider at the time how well the conference is working and how you might help it work even better?

• re-examine your own opinions and adjust them if the other person comes up with a better idea?

Simple checklists, such as those on pages 28 and 29, can stimulate reflection on peer-conference dynamics. In the first form, the students choose the skills they wish to highlight. In the second checklist, you can choose the skills you wish to emphasize, changing them periodically as students become more proficient or as different needs arise.

Parents as Collaborators

When you are thinking about involving family members remember that, in order to be fully effective, the collaborative process should remain under the writer's control. Mature student writers make decisions about content and form, drafting or filing, timing of peer/adult conferences, sharing and publishing, and submitting work for marking. They gain experience and perspective through exploratory (pre-writing) activities, peer- or adult-revision conferences, and peer- or adult-editing conferences. They are thereby enabled to revise and edit their own writing, evaluate the effectiveness of the drafting process, and evaluate the effectiveness of their own writing.

Ideally, collaboration should affirm a writer's strengths and attend to deficiencies without abrogating the writer's independence. In any collaborative situation involving adults, such as parents, guardians, or older siblings, the goal is empowerment of the individual writer. Emerging, dependent writers, of course, will be more reluctant to accept full responsibility for the decision-making aspects of the writing process. Adults need to be sensitive to an individual's comfort level with the process and encourage as much independence as the student writer is ready to accept. Supporting and assisting an emerging writer can be a complex and changeable task.

The role that parents, guardians, or older siblings play in the revising and editing processes depends very much on the individual at home and on the direction sent home by the teacher. From their mature perspectives, varied backgrounds and experience, and with their unique and intimate understanding of the individual student, parents have much to offer. They can critique with disarming appreciation, probe with just the right gentle question, clarify with a simple statement, or redirect with an apt suggestion. On the other hand, they can also take on the task of revising and editing themselves, leaving the student writer disenfranchised and dependent. Even worse, some parents might assume such a destructively critical stance that the student writer becomes discouraged, dispirited, and ultimately, reluctant to write. For these reasons, if parents, guardians, or older siblings are going to take part in revision or editing conferences at home, ensure that all of the following conditions are met:

- The student writer should willingly agree to the conferences and be prepared to lead them.
- Send home specific directions for conducting conferences to guide parental involvement (see "Revising and Editing with a Student Writer" on pages 30–31).
- All drafts with all changes from the conferences should be retained and handed in with the final draft.

Peer-conference Skills Focus

My name: _____

My partner's name: _____

Type of conference (Please check one):

Revision ☐   Editing ☐

Date of conference: _____

Three skills I applied well   Three skills I hope to improve

- _____   - _____

  _____   _____

- _____   - _____

  _____   _____

- _____   - _____

  _____   _____

Self-assessment of Peer-conference Performance

Please consider your usual performance in a peer conference and circle your choice.

A. How often do you . . .   (Always, Often, Sometimes, Not Often, Never)

- go out of your way to help the other person have
  his or her turn to speak?   **A   O   S   N/O   N**

- speak up without cutting off the other person
  or shortchanging discussion of a particular issue?   **A   O   S   N/O   N**

- indicate in your gestures, facial expressions, or
  posture that you're interested in what is being said?   **A   O   S   N/O   N**

B. How difficult is it for you to . . .   (Extremely, Very, Somewhat, Difficult at Times,
Not Difficult at All)

- go out of your way to help the other person have
  his or her turn to speak?   **E   V   S   D/T   N/D**

- speak up without cutting off the other person or
  shortchanging discussion of a particular issue?   **E   V   S   D/T   N/D**

- indicate in your gestures, facial expressions, or
  posture that you're interested in what is being said?   **E   V   S   D/T   N/D**

C. How successfully do you . . .   (Extremely, Very, Somewhat, Successfully at Times,
Not Successful at All)

- go out of your way to help the other person have
  his or her turn to speak?   **E   V   S   S/T   N/S**

- speak up without cutting off the other person or
  shortchanging discussion of a particular issue?   **E   V   S   S/T   N/S**

- indicate in your gestures, facial expressions, or
  posture that you're interested in what is being said?   **E   V   S   S/T   N/S**

Revising and Editing with a Student Writer
Guidelines for Parents, Guardians, and Older Siblings

The student writer would appreciate your assistance with revising or editing a piece of writing in the context of a conference. The writer should know what kind of help is required and be able to lead the conference. If you agree to act as a conference partner, the following suggestions will help guide you through the process.

General Guidelines

- Whoever controls the pen or pencil controls the conference and the decisions made during it. Whether revising or editing, leave the pen or pencil physically in the student's hand. Make verbal comments only.

- Revising and editing are two separate processes. Find out from the student writer the kind of conference you're enabling.

- You want to offer guidance, not give dictation. When your own words, expressions, and other language preferences start to crop up in the writing, the work is becoming yours, not the student's.

- You know your child. Keep watching for signs of frustration and discouragement. When negative feelings begin to dominate, nothing constructive can be achieved. Quickly return to some positive reinforcement and, for the time being, bring the conference to a close.

Guidelines for Revision

- If you are assisting with a revision conference, *only* discuss the content of the piece. Spelling and other usage errors will be addressed later. Please ignore these kinds of errors unless they obscure the meaning.

- One effective way of launching a revision conference is reading the material aloud. If you read the material aloud, the student writer might gain some added insight listening to his/her own words.

- The writer should have a starting point in mind for the conference, often in the form of a question or a concern about a particular aspect. Once a revision conference gets under way, however, feel free to comment on aspects of the writing you enjoyed or appreciated or parts that affected or intrigued you. You might mention how the writing involved you, what similar experiences you have had, or what the writing made you start thinking about.

- When suggesting revisions, focus on the problem rather than the solution. When in doubt, ask for clarification.

Examples:

> I'm a little confused in this section. What exactly did you mean? Can you say it in a different way to help me understand the idea?

> In paragraph three, it seems you're saying this . . . Is that what you meant?

> I noticed you used the word "nice" a number of times. Could you substitute other words to help give me a clearer picture of what you're describing?

Guidelines for Editing

- When editing, always begin with positive reinforcement. Comment on specific words spelled correctly or examples of accurate usage.

- When editing, keep the student's age, level of language ability, and grade expectations in mind. If the writing is riddled with mechanical errors, focus on only a few or a few of a similar type. Pointing out all errors in that kind of situation will only discourage the writer and inhibit learning from the errors.

- If you detect a certain kind of error, such as repeating "alot" for "a lot," point out the first example and ask the student to hunt for others.

- When editing, have a thesaurus and dictionary at hand, but don't overuse them. Looking up word after word dulls rather than sharpens usage. Besides, finding words in a dictionary can sometimes be a daunting task. If the student displays uncertainty using either reference tool, feel free to demonstrate how you would approach the task.

- Ask for clarification whenever possible and feel free to supply a certain number of corrections to keep the process from becoming stalled. You might say something like, "What word is this? Oh, I see. The reason I was confused is that 'engineer' is spelled . . ."

- Too much editing at one sitting can leave the wrong impression about the worth of the writing. If the student becomes noticeably discouraged, leave the editing and come back to it later or suggest that the student finish with a peer at school.

A Matter of Trust

As students develop an appreciation of collaboration for generating and testing ideas and for revising and editing material, they will come to feel that they belong to a community of writers. Trust is essential for this kind of writing environment to flourish. Depending on the student's age, level of confidence, and familiarity with collaborative activities, building trust may take time. Collaboration among students will develop naturally, however, as they take control of their own writing, have something to say, and realize that they need assistance to say it well.

Teachers have a more difficult task establishing themselves as collaborative partners. When the writing is completed and handed in, teachers judge its worth and assign a mark. Students are often leery, at first, of revealing a piece of writing in its formative stages to its ultimate evaluator. Teachers should make clear to students the specific role they're assuming on any given day and stick to that role. As collaborative partners, their participation reflects the assistance given to professional writers by their editors prior to publication. As students witness the nature and value of that role, trust will grow.

The role of family members in a collaborative writing process is more complex. In most cases, parents, guardians, and older siblings have already supported students in completing homework assignments, preparing projects, and studying for tests. The working relationship between family member and student has already been established through those experiences. In some cases, the role of trusted conference partner will flow naturally out of the customary working relationship; in others, the dynamic will need to be carefully directed and monitored. When teachers explain and guide such a collaborative partnership, however, family members usually respond enthusiastically. While students realize the services of another interested, trusted adult in the writing process, conferences afford family members an opportunity to interact meaningfully and positively with students about schoolwork without fear of confrontation or failure. In any mentoring situation, the mentor benefits most. Family members have much to gain from their participation in a community of writers.

CHAPTER 3

Revision Checklists

Focus on Fundamentals

This chapter, as well as Chapter 4, supplies some basic tools for teaching the revision process. It focuses on correctable stylistic flaws. A series of checklists help students spot and revise common, recurrent weaknesses. These checklists can be photocopied, reviewed with the students, and placed in their individual writing folders for easy reference. Students can use them for self-revision or in peer conferences. A brief explanation for teachers precedes each set of checklists which cover the following fundamentals: paragraphs, sentences, and word choices.

Paragraph

One or more sentences about a single topic, grouped together, and usually with an indented first line

---

Writers use paragraphs to help readers make sense of what they're reading. The simplest and most clear-cut case of paragraphing, for example, allows readers to keep track of who is talking during written conversations. In dialogues, a new paragraph signals that the speaker has changed. In this specialized case, a paragraph might range from one word to a number of sentences. As in the sample dialogue below, the first sentence of each paragraph is commonly indented to indicate where the paragraph starts. In keyboarding, the first paragraph is often indented, while succeeding paragraphs are indicated by a space between paragraphs rather than an indentation.

"Bob, how about coming over tonight and helping me with my math homework?" asked Juan.
"Sure. What time?"
"How about 7:00 p.m.?"

Paragraphs also make reading easier by dividing a relatively large section of writing into smaller, more manageable chunks. Just as a loaf of bread needs to be broken into smaller, more easily digestible pieces consumed one by one, writing is "chunked" into paragraphs to organize and highlight separate segments of thought. Although loaves of bread are usually divided into uniform slices, paragraph size varies. Since a paragraph is loosely defined as a group of related sentences dealing with a subdivision of thought, different writers will often paragraph precisely the same material in entirely different ways. Beyond the conventions for writing dialogue, inviolable rules for paragraphing are rare. Through trial and error, however, writers have developed some general guidelines. These principles are highlighted in "Paragraph Checklist for Students."

Sentence

A word or words grouped together to convey meaning,
often, but not always, containing two elements:
what you are talking about (the subject) and what you
want to say about it (the predicate)

In the endless battle against sentence fragments, teachers keep reiterating that a sentence contains two elements: what you are talking about (the subject) and what you want to say about it (the predicate). In most cases, both elements are required to preserve the essence and the clarity of each thought. Sentences can also be manipulated in a number of other ways to enhance the power and impact of what is being said. In the "Sentence Checklist for Students" on pages 36–37, several of these stylistic fundamentals are featured and explained. These principles are sometimes ignored by professional or experienced writers in search of special effects for specific purposes. In most cases, however, students should examine their writing for the following six common flaws and correct them:

1. incomplete or incomprehensible sentences
2. long or awkwardly worded sentences
3. sentences beginning with "There is" or "There are"
4. unnecessary subordinate clauses
5. weak beginnings and endings
6. not enough sentence variety

Paragraph Checklist for Students

Examine your writing in the light of the following questions to discover weaknesses in paragraphing and possible improvements:

- Are any of your paragraphs so long that you lose your place or wonder when they'll ever end? If so, where can you best break those paragraphs into smaller paragraphs?

- Are any of your paragraphs so short that the meaning seems incomplete or ideas are chopped off or the sequence of thought ends abruptly? What can you add to complete the meaning or finish the idea or sequence of thought?

- Have you used the emphatic positions of beginning and ending sentences in each paragraph to good effect? If not, how can you make your beginning and ending stronger?

- Is it clear in each paragraph what you are talking about without referring to the preceding paragraph? If not, what can you add to make the paragraph clear?

- Have you used connective words, such as *however*, *moreover*, *nevertheless*, or *on the other hand*, when appropriate? Where could they be added to create a smoother flow?

- Have you used connecting ideas to make the movement from one paragraph to another smooth and logical? If not, what ideas need to be added to link the paragraphs?

Sentence Checklist for Students

- Are any of your statement sentences incomplete in thought or incomprehensible when read by someone else?

  Examples:
  Where I left it. (draft)
  The book was right where I left it. (revision)

  Which she did last week. (draft)
  She handed in the project which she did last week. (revision)

  Though she didn't believe him. (draft)
  She had to accept his explanation even though she didn't believe him. (revision)

  Who didn't like rollerblading. (draft)
  He was one of the few people in his class who didn't like rollerblading. (revision)

On the other hand, don't confuse some of these sample sentence fragments with questions. The following questions, with wording similar to the fragments above, are perfectly correct:

  Examples:
  Where did she leave it?
  Who doesn't like rollerblading?

- Do any of your sentences seem so long or so awkwardly worded that they fail to effectively express what you wanted to say? If so, how can you reword the sentence to get at the core idea?

  Example:
  (draft)
  Even though I spend a lot of time by myself, I don't think it's a good idea to spend so much time by yourself that you get cut off from other people and start to feel lonely.
  (revised)
  When I spend too much time by myself, I start to feel lonely.

- Can you tighten up any of your sentences by eliminating "There is" or "There are"?

  Examples:
  (draft)
  There is a special story which I learned from my grandmother.
  (revised)
  I learned a special story from my grandmother.
  or
  My grandmother taught me a special story.

(draft)
There are a lot of people who don't like slow music.
(revised)
A lot of people dislike slow music.

- Can you simplify and improve sentences by removing subordinate clauses?

  Example:
  (draft)
  We danced to the music which was loud and fast.
  (revised)
  We danced to loud, fast music.

- Do you have an important word or phrase at the beginning and the end of your sentences?

  Examples:
  (draft)
  What's the best order to put words **in**?
  (revised)
  What's the best word **order**?
  (draft)
  It's about time for the game to start.
  (revised)
  The game is about to start.

- Do you use a variety of sentence structures to inject interest and an element of unpredictability into your writing?

  Example:
  I tried out for the team. I didn't make it. (draft)
  Although I tried out for the team, I didn't make it. (revision)
  I tried out for the team, but didn't make it. (revision)
  I tried out for the team; I didn't make it. (revision)

- Do you sometimes change the order of the sections in a sentence to create variety or emphasis?

  Example:
  She finally returned to school after a long illness. (draft)
  After a long illness, she finally returned to school. (revision)
  Finally, she returned to school after a long illness. (revision)
  Finally, after a long illness, she returned to school. (revision)

Word

As author Frank Smith put it, a word is a sequence of letters with a white space on either side. These small units may contain meaning by themselves or help express meaning in association with other words.

When students consider word choices, they usually think in terms of "finding a better word" or substituting a synonym. In fact, word substitution is the most commonly used student revision technique. Students need to consider other kinds of word choices to effect positive, stylistic change in their writing. A few, well-chosen words can add clarity, interest, and impact to any thought. In general, specific, concrete words from everyday language are best. Overly long, unfamiliar, or obscure words should be avoided. Students should say what they want to say as simply, directly, and straightforwardly as possible.

"Word Choice Checklist for Students" (at right) focuses on these suggestions:

- replacing neutral verbs
- changing a general phrase to a specific one
- using plural pronouns
- replacing vague words

The various student checklists in this chapter can be personalized in several ways. After they become familiar with the checklists, students can be encouraged to use check marks when revising their writing to identify instances of apt and commendable usage. They can also identify their own language tendencies, citing examples from the checklists and adding further examples from their own writing. Teachers can highlight the examples from the checklists that crop up most often in the writing from a particular class, reinforcing the checklist samples with anonymous illustrations culled from material handed in for marking. Teachers will also want to augment the checklists with additional items and stylistic patterns to make them either more comprehensive or more representative of a specific grade level or class.

Word Choice Checklist for Students

Apply the following questions and examples to your next piece of writing. Make as many of the recommended changes as you can to add clarity, interest, and impact to your word choices.

- Can you replace neutral verbs standing alone, such as *is*, *have*, or *seem* with more dynamic, vivid choices?

  Examples:
     Mrs. Turner was our Math teacher. (draft)
     Mrs. Turner taught us Math. (revision)

     From the look on her face, she seemed fatigued. (draft)
     Fatigue lined her face. (revision)

     He always has an excuse for being late. (draft)
     He always excuses his lateness. (revision)

- Will changing a general phrase with a specific one strengthen the word picture?

  Example:
     A girl was talking to the class. (draft)
     Anika, the class president, addressed her Grade 8 classmates. (revision)

- Can you replace the awkward, singular pronoun phrase *she* or *he* with a plural pronoun?

  Example:
     Each person should do what she or he thinks best. (draft)
     People should do what they think best. (revision)

- Can you replace vague words, such as *thing* or *something*, with specific nouns?

  Examples:

     She had a thing to do after school. (draft)
     She had an errand to run after school. (revision)

     He tripped over something hidden in the grass. (draft)
     He tripped over a large rock hidden in the grass. (revision)

CHAPTER 4

Peer-revision Models

Windows into Revision Conferences

This chapter offers a series of models designed to demonstrate and implement the principles of peer revision. Revision in pairs or in small groups is a powerful writing technique and a mainstay of writer's workshop or writing process programs. Once students have revised their own material to the best of their abilities, they turn to peer-revision conferences to continue the process. Many students, however, are unsure of their roles in these conferences or even what they're supposed to say or do in them. They need the opportunity to experience a few successful conferences in action to fully understand how to shape and control the technique for their own purposes. The revision models in this chapter act as windows into these conferences to demonstrate and illuminate the peer-revision process in a practical way.

Students usually work in pairs or, sometimes, in small groups. At the beginning of a conference, students read aloud a student draft and then critique it. The reading aloud may be done by the author, by the peer-revision partner, or by a group member. All members, including the author, must be present as the piece is read aloud.

The author usually starts the discussion by voicing a question or concern about the writing. As the discussion continues, the author makes notes about the points being made. The author takes the different perspectives into consideration during the next draft, but is under no compulsion to follow the advice expressed in the conference. Some student authors like to have two or three different revision conferences before dealing with the various viewpoints in the next draft.

Although the technique is relatively simple to explain, it is decidedly difficult to implement. Student authors, first, are reluctant to take control of the conference. They need to be taught to direct and shape the conference to fit their needs. They also need to take physical control of the marking pen. If anything need to be noted on their draft, they should do it. Their revision partners, on the other hand, are initially reluctant to offer considered criticism or constructive suggestions, opting instead for enthusiastic approval, regardless of the quality. Even when teachers are able to convince their students about the value and effectiveness of peer-revision conferences, many students are stalled about what to expect, what to say, what to do, and how to offer supportive criticism at the same time.

A potent technique for teaching the practical workings of such peer conferences is modelling. The teacher places a sample piece of writing on an overhead and talks the students through a sample conference. The demonstration shows how an author might begin a peer conference, what might be said about the piece, the kinds of notes the author might make as the conference progresses, and the kinds of changes the author might make in the next draft based on the conference input. While such modelling is unquestionably a powerful learning/teaching tool, few teachers have the resources, experience, or confidence to attempt the technique unaided. The models that follow are designed to fill that need, taking teachers step-by-step through the process and supplying whatever resources are required. These models of peer-revision conferences are divided into eight series:

1. Revising a prose narrative 1 (intermediate)
2. Revising a prose narrative 2 (junior)
3. Revising an essay 1 (intermediate)
4. Revising an essay 2 (junior/intermediate)
5. Revising a poem 1 (intermediate)
6. Revising a poem 2 (junior/intermediate)
7. Revising a prose narrative into a poem (intermediate)
8. Revising a project (junior/intermediate)

Each series begins with some background for the teacher and a set of directions which indicate the need for overhead transparencies or photocopies of the student pages and their precise use. Full-class, small-group, and individual activities are included. In some cases, the teacher is required to model on an overhead projector how the student author might mark a draft in response to peer comments.

A successful peer-revision conference requires participation from both the writer and the responder to keep it relevant. Depending on the individual student and the needs of the piece of writing, a revision conference might include two, three or, occasionally, four or more responders. Most conferences are best handled and seem most productive, especially with relatively inexperienced writers, when only one or two responders are present. At the outset, the writer should try to direct the responder in some specific way. Rather than asking what's good about the piece or how the responder would change it, the writer needs to draw attention to whatever he or she is grappling with in the writing or feeling uneasy about. As well, if the writer reads the piece of material aloud, strengths and weaknesses are sometimes more easily apprehended by the listeners, including the writer. The responders strive to give the writer first-hand glimpses into how readers react to the material rather than attempting to "fix" or "improve" the material. The writer tries to focus these personal reactions.

Two student guidelines follow. "Peer-conference Guidelines for the Student Author" supplies student authors with specific ways to prepare for a peer conference. "Guidelines for Peer-revision Conferences" outlines the roles that responder and writer assume once the conference starts. These guidelines can be used before or after the teacher modelling, depending on your assessment of how they best meet the needs of a particular class.

Peer-conference Guidelines for the Student Author

As the writer, you are in charge of any conferences about what you've written. Instead of handing your work over to someone else and asking them what they think of it, try to direct the responders in some specific way. Draw their attention to any areas you're having trouble with or are uncertain about or need help with. Ask a conference partner to read your draft aloud. You will appreciate your piece in a different way when you hear the words come out of someone else's mouth. You will also be able to identify strengths and weakness more easily hearing the material read aloud. Ask each conference partner to give you a first-hand glimpse into how a reader reacts to the material rather than concentrating right away on attempting to fix or improve the writing. The following suggestions will help you prepare for the peer conference.

Prior to a peer conference . . .

- Read your piece aloud to yourself to hear how it sounds.

- Put check marks on your draft wherever you identify a strength in the writing, for example, a striking phrase or vivid use of language, an effective title or opening, or a persuasive argument.

- Put question marks on your draft wherever you would like help or an opinion. You might note items to rephrase, take out, add to, or rearrange. Write down some specific questions about your draft that you would like answered based on the question marks you've placed on your draft.

- Ask a peer to read your draft and discuss it with you.

- Guide the discussion by drawing out your partners' reactions and getting answers to your own questions.

- During the conference, make notes on your draft as reminders about what to do when you tackle the next draft.

Guidelines for Peer-revision Conferences

As you discuss a piece of writing, keep in mind that both the responder and the writer have certain responsibilities in the revision process. The following questions highlight those responsibilities.

The Responder	The Writer
What, specifically, has the writer asked you to think about?	What have you asked your responder to do?
How did you first respond to the material? What happened in your mind as you read? What aspects intrigued or attracted you?	What impact did the material have on the responder? How does this reaction compare with the impact you expected?
What, if anything, confused you as you read? What ideas or events were unclear? What, if anything, was left out or seemed out of place?	What will you have to take out, put in, change, or rearrange?
How did you respond to the opening and closing, the language, the development of ideas, or to the pace? What people or events did you want to know more about?	How can the responder help you further? What more do you want to know?

Series 1: Revising a Prose Narrative 1 (Intermediate)

> *ordinary*
> **Prose narrative**
>
> A form of writing in which a person tells a story, actual or fictional

The three models that follow these directions offer a revision sequence for hands-on practice. Please feel free to photocopy or create overhead transparencies for classroom use.

How to use Model 1A: First responses

Direct the class discussion using an overhead transparency of the page. Explain that the left-hand side of the page shows the first draft of a student narrative. The right-hand side features real responses of other students during a revision conference. Although the first-draft prose narrative contains a variety of spelling and usage errors, since the students were focusing on revision, most of these errors were ignored. The errors were addressed only if they obscured the meaning.

Read aloud the narrative and then mention that before the peer conference, the student author seemed satisfied with the draft. The author's guiding questions were "Is the title O.K.?" and "How can I make the opening better?" One by one, address the response comments, emphasizing that these comments were made orally to the author and, that during a revision conference, the author takes responsibility for making notes on the written work. Using an overhead marker, mark the left-hand side of the page as the student author might have done to note the comments made by the revision partners. (Please see "Teacher Marking Guideline," page 47.) After discussing the actual responses, invite other revision suggestions from the class. These additional responses should be noted on the page.

How to use Model 1B: Further refining

The left-hand side of the page shows the original first draft of the narrative from Model 1A. The right-hand side of the page features the second draft of the narrative. Either photocopy this page or create an overhead transparency. Discuss the material as a class group, in revision pairs, or in small groups. Directions for the discussion are on the top of the page.

How to use Model 1C: What would you say?

The left-hand side of the page presents another student-written first-draft narrative. Either photocopy this page or create an overhead transparency. Direct students to conduct a revision conference either as a class group or in smaller groups. In the full-class group, act as surrogate author and mark the narrative in response to the revision comments and suggestions. If smaller groups are used, designate a student from each group as scribe.

Down by the Beach!

I walk along the beach on a mild and foggy day. I look up in the sky and see how the doves fly with there wings fully extended up so high. As I look at the doves I see the sea, not even a ripple, as flat as can be. The sand along the beach was like waves on the sea, all tossed and turned. The boats by the dock were all tied up, just floating still, like parked cars. I turned around and looked at my footprints in the sand, they were fiathing away as I looked farther on. Everytime when I want to be free, I just go down to the beach and sit by the sea.

Response: What is your story really about? Can you make your title more specific?

Response: How come you're there? How do you feel?

Response: Usually you see seagulls by the ocean. I think it's strange to see doves there. Why not have them coming in and out of the mist?

Response: The rhyming in the story sounds funny because it's not a poem. You start listening to the rhyme and not what you're saying.

Response: This is fantastic description. I really like the sand looking all wavy and the boats like parked cars.

Response: If you made a new paragraph around here, maybe the ending would be emphasized.

Response: Why not mention the footprints at the beginning? That way we know about them when you mention them again. This part seems sad.

Response: "Fiathing"? Did you mean "fading"?

Response: Is this what the story's about? The footprints fading away before didn't seem like the same kind of feeling. You've got rhyming in the sentence again.

Other Responses:

Model 1A: Teacher Marking Guide

Down by the Beach!

— title more specific?

— seagulls in mist?

I walk along the beach on a

— why there? *— feeling?*

mild and foggy day. I look up in the

seagulls?

sky and see how the (doves) fly with

there wings fully extended up so

— rhyme?

high. As I look at the (doves) I see

the sea, not even a ripple, as flat as

— rhyme?

can be. The sand along the beach

was like waves on the sea, all

tossed and turned. The boats by the

dock were all tied up, just floating

still, like parked cars. I turned

around and looked at my footprints

— footprints at beginning

in the sand, they were fiathing away

fading

as I looked farther on. Everytime

ending?

when I want to be (free,) I just go

down to the beach and sit by the

(sea.)

rhyme?

Response: What is your story really about? Can you make your title more specific?

Response: How come you're there? How do you feel?

Response: Usually you see seagulls by the ocean. I think it's strange to see doves there. Why not have them coming in and out of the mist?

Response: The rhyming in the story sounds funny because it's not a poem. You start listening to the rhyme and not what you're saying.

Response: This is fantastic description. I really like the sand looking all wavy and the boats like parked cars.

Response: If you made a new paragraph around here, maybe the ending would be emphasized.

Response: Why not mention the footprints at the beginning? That way we know about them when you mention them again. This part seems sad.

Response: "Fiathing"? Did you mean "fading"?

Response: Is this what the story's about? The footprints fading away before didn't seem like the same kind of feeling. You've got rhyming in the sentence again.

Other Responses:

Model 1B: Further Refining

On the left side of this page is the first draft of "Down by the Beach!" On the right side is the second draft.
   a. Identify the revisions. Do you agree or disagree with them? Explain.
   b. What changes would you suggest for the third draft? Why?

Down by the Beach!

I walk along the beach on a mild and foggy day. I look up in the sky and see how the doves fly with there wings fully extended up so high. As I look at the doves I see the sea, not even a ripple, as flat as can be. The sand along the beach was like waves on the sea, all tossed and turned. The boats by the dock were all tied up, just floating still, like parked cars. I turned around and looked at my footprints in the sand, they were fiathing away as I looked farther on. Everytime when I want to be free, I just go down to the beach and sit by the sea.

Footprints

The beach is deserted on this mild and foggy morning. As I walk along the sand, I leave a solitary trail of footprints behind me. Up in the sky, flocks of seagulls fly in and out of the mist with their wings fully extended. Below the seagulls, the sea is so flat there isn't even a ripple. The sand along the beach was like waves, all tossed and turned. The boats by the dock were all tied up, just floating still, like parked cars.

When I want to be free, I go down to the beach. But today I just feel sad. I turn around and look at my footprints in the sand. They were fading away. I keep on walking.

Model 1C: What Would You Say?

The Football Game

Responses:

Today was the day my dad promised to take me to the football game. When we got there you could hear the cheer-leader yelling. People were talking in the lobby about the game. You could hear people slurping down hot coffee and smell the hot buttered popcorn being made. Out in the stands the coffee smelt so strong you oculd taste it. I had a perfect view of the players on the field. The players were getting ready for the kick-off. people were yelling for their favorite team. I could barely hear my dad talking to me for the people shouting. Everybody roared at the first kick-off.

Series 2: Revising a Prose Narrative 2 (Junior)

> ### Sentence combining
>
> A teaching technique in which students build a single complex sentence from a series of simple sentences

Teachers strive to help their students improve their writing in a variety of ways. Engaging in writing, obviously, heads the list of effective approaches authenticated by research, followed by reading, the study of models, and sentence combining. Writer's workshop or writing process classrooms promote daily writing in class. Daily self-selected reading in class is the complement to an effective writing program, as long as students have regular opportunities to respond to the reading in personally significant ways and to discuss the reading with someone else. The study of models can occur in a variety of contexts, from listening to and discussing read-alouds to examining and analyzing exemplary writing samples. Finally, sentence combining offers a rewriting skill that students can practise and transfer to their own writing.

The sentence-combining technique is relatively simple to apply: a series of basic sentences are combined in a single complex sentence. Depending on how the sentences are manipulated, a variety of end results are possible. The final sentences, however, must be correctly and effectively structured. Joining a series of simple sentences with *and*, for example, would be correct, but hardly effective. The following sample demonstrates how the approach unfolds:

Sample series:

> The gym was filled with students.
> They were in the gym for an assembly.
> They were laughing.
> They were yelling.
> They were hot.
> They were tired.
> The assembly was late starting.

Some sample combinations:

- The gym was filled with hot and tired students who began laughing and yelling when the assembly was late starting.
- Hot and tired, the students filling the gym began to laugh and yell when the assembly was late starting.
- Since the assembly was late starting and they were hot and tired, the students filling the gym were laughing and yelling.

The technique is ideally presented as a problem-solving exercise for small groups. Some teachers ask a scribe from each group to write the sentence combinations on an overhead projector transparency with a marker. The various sentences from each group can then be examined and discussed in a large-group context. When students are familiar with the technique, they enjoy creating their own series of simple sentences and exchanging them to be solved by another group.

Keep in mind that the goal is always to turn the students back to their own writing. A little practice out of the context of the drafting process goes a long way. When students realize the possibilities in sentence manipulation, they're ready to draft their own writing with new eyes.

The "Sentence Combining" practice sheet (page 52) will get students started on the technique. A model prose narrative then allows the students to transfer and apply the learning to an actual piece of writing. Please feel free to photocopy or create overhead transparencies for classroom use.

How to Use Model 2A: Revising Through Sentence Combining

The left-hand side of the page contains a student-written prose narrative. The narrative includes a number of simple sentences. Display the narrative on an overhead projector and read it aloud to the class. Ask the students to identify groups of simple sentences that could usefully be combined. Circle these groups of sentences using an overhead marker. The first group is already circled and a sample combined sentence is found on the right-hand side of the page. When all the sentences have been identified, ask the students to combine each group of sentences into one correct, effective sentence. They can do this activity individually or in small groups. They should then rewrite the narrative with the combined sentences substituted for the originals. The narratives from volunteer individuals or groups can be read aloud and discussed.

Sentence Combining

Although short, simple sentences can be used effectively in a story, too many of them can make the writing seem repetitive, choppy, and disjointed. The challenge in the following exercise is to create one correct and effective sentence out of each series of short, basic sentences. Some series can be combined in more than one way. Find as many effective combinations as you can for each group of sentences.

1. I have my own phone.
   It's a cell-phone.
   I take it almost everywhere.
   I can't take it to school.

2. The teacher taught English.
   The teacher was nice.
   The teacher assigned a lot of homework.
   The homework was hard.
   The teacher always did that.

3. I watched T.V. all day Saturday.
   I watched T.V. all Saturday night.
   I watched anything that was on.
   I did that every Saturday.
   The T.V. was in my room.
   I watched T.V. instead of doing my homework.

4. I was walking to the mall.
   I was walking slowly.
   I just had a fight with my brother.
   I felt sad.

Model 2A: Revising Through Sentence Combining

Once there was a leprechaun. He was short and wore a green suit and green hat. He lived in a dark forest. One day he was walking. A man was passing by. The man saw the leprechaun. The man got out his net and caught the leprechaun. He put a rope around the leprechaun's waist. The man was a robber. He was looking for a leprechaun to tell him where the gold was buried. The man asked the leprechaun to tell him where the gold was buried. The leprechaun was very clever and tricky. The leprechaun said yes. The man followed the leprechaun. The leprechaun was very smart and took him the wrong way. When the leprechaun stopped by a big tree, he told the man to start digging. He said that the gold was in the ground beside the tree. The man was excited. He dropped the rope and started to dig. He dug and dug and dug. He didn't find anything. Then he got angry. He looked around for the leprechaun. The leprechaun had vanished. The man dug and dug and dug but he never found any gold. The leprechaun had tricked him. Nobody ever came to the dark forest again. Nobody ever saw the leprechaun again.

1. Once upon a time, a short leprechaun in a green suit and hat was walking in the dark forest where he lived.

Series 3: Revising an Essay 1 (Intermediate)

> ### Essay
> A relatively brief literary composition, usually in prose, providing the author's views on a particular topic

From the Intermediate grades on, students encounter a curious exception to the rule of function preceding form: the essay. This type of composition is often presented as a kind of all-purpose container into which students are encouraged to pour their thoughts about various issues.

Many teachers customarily introduce essay structure in the same way they were taught to organize their arguments when they were students: the "hamburger" paragraph. In this long-standing conceit, a body of supporting statements of fact, evidence, or explanation is squeezed between a topic sentence that sets out the main idea and a conclusion that tries to answer the question, So what? Some teachers refine the approach even further by insisting on a five-sentence "hamburger" essay: an introduction, three supporting facts, and a conclusion. This "hamburger" approach to essay writing caught on for several reasons. The format is easy to teach and easy to mark; moreover, the structure mimics the essential essay characteristics.

Unfortunately, this kind of rigid, restrictive, and simplistic approach tends to inhibit the development of effective argumentation. The form of an essay must necessarily remain flexible enough to follow the contours of a specific argument.

Intrinsic to successful argumentation are the linkages in content from statement of thesis through substantiating propositions, a chain of reasoning, and a logical consistency that produces a unified whole. This kind of argumentation usually includes

- an introduction leading to an explicit statement of the position to be argued;
- a series of arguments, sometimes accompanied by substantiating illustrations;
- sometimes, a refutation of counter-arguments; and
- a conclusion restating the argument.

More characteristic of student exposition is the informal essay; basically, a lot of information about a specific topic. Left to their own devices and inclinations, most students will research, compile, and restate personally relevant facts about a topic, such as wrestling or an entertainer. Less often, they might attempt an argument about the merits of wrestling as a legitimate sport or whether popular entertainers have a responsibility to act as role models.

The following student guidelines offer some specific direction regarding the essay. Once again, these guidelines can be used before or after the teacher modelling, depending on the teacher's assessment of how they best meet class needs. The first student guideline supplies student authors with specific ways to prepare for writing an essay. The second student guideline offers suggestions for beginning a peer-revision conference on an essay.

Student Guideline for Generating Essay Ideas

If you aren't sure what you want to say, you'll have difficulty writing an essay. Clear thinking propels clear writing.

Sometimes, you require some pre-writing activities to clarify your thoughts. You could talk about your thoughts and opinions with someone else, for example, or read more on the subject. Informal writing activities, such as making a spontaneous journal entry or jotting down some stream-of-consciousness notes, may also help you uncover how you feel about an issue.

To generate ideas for writing, some people like to brainstorm either alone or with a group. Brainstorming an essay topic can reveal an unexpected range and depth of opinion and argument, pinpoint contentious areas requiring more research, and establish the tone.

Brainstorming

Generating a list of examples, ideas, or questions to illustrate, expand, or explore a central idea or topic

---

Brainstorming suggestions:

- Appoint one person as scribe. Participants offer suggestions in turn as ideas occur.

- Get as many ideas as possible; quantity is important.

- Record all ideas — even zany ones.

- Focus on collecting ideas only. Don't discuss or evaluate them now.

- Feel free to expand on someone else's idea.

After the brainstorming is completed, go back over the ideas and check off the ones you think are worthwhile. Group these ideas according to any characteristics that stand out, such as pro or con, fact versus opinion, or most important to least important.

Once you, yourself, understand what you want to say, you are ready to help someone else understand what you think. You are going to set out your arguments in such a way as to lead your reader into agreeing with your point of view.

Student Guideline for Writing and Revising an Essay

A good essay will be structured logically and sequentially. Keep these suggestions in mind as you begin to write:

• Set out precisely what you are planning to investigate and what you hope to prove.

• Set up a series of proofs or arguments to persuade the reader.

• Conclude by restating whatever you've proven in a dramatic, emphatic, or memorable way.

Once you have a draft essay that seems persuasive to you, seek responses to it from someone else. After your peer partner has read aloud your essay, discuss it. With an essay, you can ask your partner a set of specific questions:

• What is the main point I'm trying to make?

• What arguments did you find most convincing?

• What arguments for or against can you add?

• Did you agree with me in the end? Why or why not?

• What ideas would you switch around?

At this point, review the responses to your essay, paying particular attention to the responses that surprised or puzzled you. Decide which of your partner's ideas to adopt, which arguments to clarify or bolster, and where you need to rephrase your thoughts. Use these decisions to guide your next draft.

The three models that follow these directions offer a revision sequence for hands-on practice. Please feel free to photocopy or create overhead transparencies for classroom use.

How to use Model 3A: Thinking it through

Direct the class discussion using an overhead transparency of the page. Explain that the left-hand side of the page shows the first draft of a student essay. The right-hand side features the responses of other students during a revision conference. Although the first-draft essay contains a variety of spelling and usage errors, since the students were focusing on revision, most of these errors were ignored. The errors were addressed only if they obscured the meaning.

Read aloud the essay and then mention that the author's guiding questions were, "I think maybe the opening is too long. What do you think?" and "Can you think of any other ideas for or against spanking that I could use?" One by one, address the response comments, emphasizing that these comments were made orally to the author and, that during a revision conference, the author is responsible for making notes on the written work. Using an overhead marker, mark the left-hand side of the page as the student author might have done to note the comments made by the revision partners. (Please see "Teacher Marking Guide," page 59.) After dealing with the actual responses, invite other revision suggestions from the class, especially pertaining to the ending and possible additional arguments. These additional responses should be noted on the page.

How to use Model 3B: What would you add?

The left-hand side of the page shows the second draft of the essay from Model 3A, minus the ending The right-hand side of the page has space for additional arguments and an ending as assigned the students in Model 3A. You can either photocopy this page or create an overhead transparency. The discussion can be conducted as a class group or in revision pairs or small groups. Direct students to add whatever arguments will produce the most persuasive essay, as well as a strong ending.

How to use Model 3C: Responding practice

The left-hand side of the page provides another student-written first-draft essay. Photocopy this page or create an overhead transparency. Direct students, either as a whole class or in smaller groups, to conduct a revision conference. If the conference is conducted with the aid of an overhead transparency, act as surrogate author and mark the essay in response to the revision comments and suggestions. If smaller groups are used, designate a student from each group as scribe.

We Shouldn't Be Spanked as Teenagers

I would say that we shouldn't be spanked as teenagers, because I am a teenager and I don't like to get spanked and not only that but when your a teenager you are more grown up and we know when we do something wrong, so we won't do it again. Instead of getting spanked our parents could ground us "because it doesn't hurt as much", for one thing. But you know they also could take something away from us for a "little" while as long as it isn't our skate boards of course.

But as we all know not everyone agrees with us. They say we should be spanked because we know when we are doing something wrong, but will we do it again most likely. Than when they ground us, that doesn't work they say they always get out of it some way. When it comes to taking something from us, we always get it back in less than a day.

So I still say that we shouldn't get spanked as teenagers well after all you were a teenager at one time.

Response: You're right. The first sentence seems too long. Why not take out the part that just repeats the title? Why not tell why you don't like to be spanked? The part about being grown up is a separate part. That could be a different sentence.

Response: Grounding doesn't hurt physically, but it hurts in other ways. Maybe if you showed how it does hurt, then someone might use it instead.

Response: Taking away privileges is a big thing with my parents. You make it kind of funny and I like that, but you should show that it's a big thing, too.

Response: Why not end your second sentence after "wrong"? That way your next point is more important.

Response: If grounding and privileges don't work, it's their fault. They need to do what they say they're going to do. Anyway, my parents make sure the punishment sticks!

Response: (Other arguments pro or con?)

Response: (Ending?)

We Shouldn't Be Spanked as Teenagers

~~I would say that we shouldn't be spanked as teenagers, because~~ I am a teenager and₂ I don't like to get spanked, *why not* and not only that but when your a teenager you are more grown up and we know when we do something wrong, so we won't do it again. Instead of getting spanked our parents could ground us, *— how does it hurt* ? "because it doesn't hurt as much", for one thing. *big thing* But you know they also could take something away from us for a "little" while as long as it isn't our skate boards of course.

But as we all know not everyone agrees with us. They say we should be spanked because we know when we are doing something wrong, *but* will we do it again most likely. Than when they ground us, that doesn't work they say they always get out of it some way. When it comes to taking something from us, we always get it back in less than a day. *— parents' fault!*

So I still say that we shoudn't get spanked as teenagers well after all you were a teenager at one time.

Response: You're right. The first sentence seems too long. Why not take out the part that just repeats the title? Why not tell why you don't like to be spanked? The part about being grown up is a separate part. That could be a different sentence.

Response: Grounding doesn't hurt physically, but it hurts in other ways. Maybe if you showed how it does hurt, then someone might use it instead.

Response: Taking away privileges is a big thing with my parents. You make it kind of funny and I like that, but you should show that it's a big thing, too.

Response: Why not end your second sentence after "wrong"? That way your next point is more important.

Response: If grounding and privileges don't work, it's their fault. They need to do what they say they're going to do. Anyway, my parents make sure the punishment sticks!

Response: (Other arguments pro or con?)

Response: (Ending?)

We Shouldn't Be Spanked as Teenagers

I am a teenager and I don't like to get spanked. A spanking is like getting beaten up. Strangers get put in jail if they beat you up. Why should your parents be different? Besides, when your a teenager you are more grown up. We know when we do something wrong and the next time we won't do it again. Our parents could ground us instead of spanking us. It doesn't hurt physically, but it still hurts. When you can't be with your friends, it feels like your in prison. Taking away privileges like T.V. or the phone or the computer hurts, too. Let's hope they don't take away our skate boards of course.

But as we all know not everyone agrees with us. They say we should be spanked because we know when we are doing something wrong. Will we do it again even if we're spanked? Most likely. Than when they ground us, that doesn't work because they say we always get out of it some way. When it comes to taking something from us, we always get it back in less than a day. Isn't that their fault? They should do what they say.
(Ending missing)

Additional responses:
(In this column, add other arguments where you think they would fit best.)

Ending: (Please add your ending here.)

Model 3C: Responding Practice

Stop Seal Hunting!

Can you imagine how many seals and especially baby ones die every year? It's unbelievable! The hunters only think about money and don't even think about the life the seals want to live. I can't believe how those savage hunters can just walk up to a seal and club it to death. Seals want to live too!!!! Animals have hearts and minds and they know how to think. They can feel pain. If you killed a human, you'd be punished and animals are just a little different from us. Suppose seals came up to people and clubbed them to death and took their skin. That's just it. They don't. They just want to live in peace. Humans don't need to wear fur. They have their own protection like clothes. Animals have their own protection. It's fur and it's theirs! And no one should take that from them and they don't take our clothes away and they don't bother us and why can't people leave them alone. If everybody helps, we can all live in peace!

Responses:

Descriptive essay

A relatively brief literary composition, usually in prose, offering a word picture, rich in details appealing to the senses, of a character, an incident, or a setting

---

We don't use a lot of descriptive language in our everyday lives. Rich and colorful description seems to belong to a written tradition appreciated by many, but practised by very few. The kind of specific, descriptive details that flesh out the people and places in the novels we read are customarily missing in our daily conversations and e-mail interactions. Instead, as adults, we often depend on the fact of shared experiences as a kind of descriptive shorthand. Since so many of our friends and colleagues have seen the autumn leaves or experienced city life or witnessed a particular kind of sporting event, we cultivate all-purpose descriptors, referring to the "amazing" colors, the "incredible" traffic, or a "great" game. As students verbally share personal experiences each day with their peers, they also depend on much "mind-reading" from their friends to illuminate their stories. Since they inhabit a mutual environment with mutual friends with mutual interests, they can fill in the essential details from sparse cues. "Helen dissed Frank in the lunchroom" needs little embellishment to stimulate full understanding and high intrigue.

Developmental factors compound the issue for students. When they write about something they have experienced first-hand, they have no trouble telling where they were, who they were with, and what happened. Adding the descriptive details that could bring the experience to life for another person, however, is quite another matter. Looking through another's eyes to imagine the kind of sensory information and imagery necessary to truly share an experience with another is a mature, complex, and sophisticated skill that slowly evolves and develops over time. A young person, however, is developmentally defined by egocentricity. The younger the students, the more likely they are to assume that the world sees everything through their eyes. Moreover, since the simplest reference to the episode stimulates a wealth of images in their own minds, students assume that the same pictures pop up in other people's minds from their simple, bare-bones account. The sharper and more vivid the experience, in fact, the less likely students are to enrich or illuminate their account of that experience. As they write about an incident, they relive a palpable range of emotions and they assume the reader does as well. The challenge with students is to help them understand how huge the gulf is between writers and readers and to appreciate the kind of essential description needed to bridge that gap.

The four models that follow these directions offer a revision sequence for hands-on practice. Please feel free to photocopy or create overhead transparencies for classroom use.

How to use Model 4A: First draft, first responses

Direct the class discussion using an overhead transparency of the page. Explain that the left-hand side of the page shows the first draft of a student descriptive essay. The right-hand side features the responses of other students during a revision conference. Although the first-draft essay contains a variety of spelling and usage errors, since the students were focusing on revision, these errors were ignored.

Read aloud the essay and then mention that the guiding question from the author was, "What kind of thing do you want to know more about?" One by one, address the response comments, emphasizing that these comments were made orally to the author and, that during a revision conference, the author is responsible for making notes on the written work. After dealing with the actual responses, invite the students to identify possible descriptive details the author might add and indicate on the overhead where these additions would be placed. Then move on to Model 4B.

How to use Model 4B: Second draft, part 1

The left-hand side of the page shows the first part of the second draft of an essay, "Waterskiing," with the actual added descriptive details highlighted. The right-hand side of the page features the original student responses. After reading aloud the essay from an overhead transparency, move on to Model 4C.

How to use Model 4C: Second draft, part 2 — your turn

The left-hand side of the page contains the rest of the first draft of the essay "Waterskiing." Photocopy the page. Ask the students, working in small groups, to rewrite it, using the responses as a guide and adding the descriptive details they think will create a more specific and concrete word picture. One student can be designated scribe for each group. When the groups are finished, ask a volunteer from each group to read aloud the new version of the second part of the essay. Solicit from the class particularly effective additions from each group's efforts.

How to use Model 4D: First draft practice

The left-hand side of the page presents another student-written first-draft descriptive essay. Either photocopy this page or create an overhead transparency. Direct the students, either as a whole class or in smaller groups, to ask the questions that will guide the writer to add the details needed to bring the essay to life. If the conference is conducted with the aid of an overhead transparency, act as surrogate author and write the questions on the right-hand side of the page. If smaller groups are used, designate a student from each group to act as scribe. After reviewing the responses, direct the students to rewrite the essay in their own individual ways, adding their own descriptive details. These essays can be shared and discussed orally.

Waterskiing

When I was watching my uncle waterskiing last summer I thought I could do it no problem but it's not as easy as it looks. All of a sudden I was in the water with the skis on my feet and the rope was coming around. I grabbed the rope and suddenly I was dragged through the water and almost drowned because I didn't pull myself up fast enough. The second time around I was pulled up right away but I had my skis leaned to far forward so when I started going faster I went flying through the air in one direction and my skis went in the other direction and when I landed I hit the water so hard. The third time I got up right away and leaned the right way and I was doing okay until I had to turn and go over a wave and I hit the wave and went flying through the air again. I didn't do any more skiing that day because the fall really spooked me. I still have a lot to learn but I better not rush it or I'll end up killing myself!

Response: Was he doing tricks and stuff? Where were you? What was the water like?

Response: What happened? Did you swallow water? Did you go under? Did someone have to rescue you?

Response: Wow! Did you land on your head or what? Did you get dragged again? What did it feel like? Weren't you scared?

Response: Is it like skateboarding or snowboarding? How fast were you going? Did you hurt yourself when you landed? Wasn't your uncle scared about getting you hurt?

Response: What do you mean by "spooked"? How was it worse the third time?

Waterskiing

When I was watching my uncle waterskiing **at the lake** last summer I thought I could do it no problem. **He just sailed over the water and he looked like he was gliding on air.** But I found out it's not as easy as it looks. All of a sudden I was in the **cold, choppy** water with the skis on my feet and the rope was coming around. I grabbed the rope and suddenly **my arms felt like they were being pulled out of their sockets** and I was dragged through the water. **I let go of the rope and went under the water and I was choking and coughing with water in my mouth and nose.** I almost drowned because I didn't pull myself up fast enough. **My uncle came around with the boat and got my skis and I told him I was o.k. after I rested for a minute or so.**

Response: Was he doing tricks and stuff? Where were you? What was the water like?

Response: What happened? Did you swallow water? Did you go under? Did someone have to rescue you?

Waterskiing

The second time around I was pulled up right away but I had my skis leaned to far forward so when I started going faster I went flying through the air in one direction and my skis went in the other direction and when I landed I hit the water so hard. The third time I got up right away and leaned the right way and I was doing okay until I had to turn and go over a wave and I hit the wave and went flying through the air again. I didn't do any more skiing that day because the fall really spooked me. I still have a lot to learn but I better not rush it or I'll end up killing myself!

Response: Wow! Did you land on your head or what? Did you get dragged again? What did it feel like? Weren't you scared?

Response: Is it like skateboarding or snowboarding? How fast were you going? Did you hurt yourself when you landed? Wasn't your uncle scared about getting you hurt?

Response: What do you mean by "spooked"? How was it worse the third time?

Rollerblading

Responses:

Everybody says that rollerblading is easy but I sure didn't find it easy. I even had trouble at the store when I was trying different kinds on. I got some cool wrist guards but my mom bought me knee pads and elbow pads and even a helmet! I tried to tell her nobody wore those. She wants me to look like a geek and have everybody laughing at me.

So then I went into the garage so I could try them out and nobody could see me. It was awful! I kept falling and falling. I wished that they sold butt-guards! Like I couldn't even stand up without holding on to something. If I crouched down really low I could sort of step and roll abit. The last time I fell I hurt my wrist and it got all puffy and sore. I told my mom to take the blades back and she didn't get all her money back and she's mad at me. I don't know why people tell you somethings easy when its not.

Series 5: Revising a Poem 1 (Intermediate)

> ### Poem
>
> A composition in which word images are selected and arranged to create an especially vivid, powerful, or beautiful impression on the listener or reader

The song-like, rhyming verse that stresses musicality, inventive imagery, and intriguing juxtapositions of the real and the make-believe, regardless of meaning, are a child's first love. Even in the most skilful of hands, however, rhyming poetry is difficult to create. When poets shape language to suit their purposes, they choose from a number of variations for the most penetrating or entertaining effect. Rhyme, however, limits the number of choices for end-of-line words. On the other hand, rhyme and rhythm can imbue a work with essential energy and distinctive attributes that can facilitate the message, tone, or purpose of the work. The skilful poet strikes a delicate balance between the benefits of rhyme and rhythm and the limitations of these conventions. The intensely crafted nature of rhyming poetry invests language with special power, grace, and beauty. Its heightened elements allow children to more easily experience and appreciate the qualities of language that affect listeners emotionally. Ironically, however, the first poetry that catches and captures a child's ear and imagination is the most difficult to create. Obviously, young children possess an extremely limited vocabulary when compared with that of the poets whose work they read and to whom they listen.

Although adults feel the emotional power of rhyming poetry, for example, in popular song lyrics, they respond to and make use of poetry with a different sensibility. Adults see poetry as a finely honed vehicle for thought and feeling and as a means by which they try to make sense of and cope with the world and their lives. With adults, the form or structure of a poem grows out of its content or meaning. What a poem says determines how it's said. Whether or not a poem rhymes, scans, or is set in lines and verse are characteristics that no longer dominate the genre or even form the criteria for judging a poem's worth. Instead, each poem is regarded as a unique creation defined by the intent and vision of the poet and judged by its intellectual and emotional impact. A teacher's main task in this area is to assist the developmental factors that allow children to grow into an expanded understanding of the role and purpose of poetry at the same time as they are growing into an expanded facility with the language.

As students grow and experience more and more of the physical world, they have increasingly more to say about that world. At the same time, they are becoming more aware of their inner world and the relationships that link the two worlds. The potent emotions that so forcefully color their lives form a natural and compelling conduit into the world of poetry. Although optic and concrete poetry and the many kinds of pattern poems, such as cinquain and haiku, have roles to play with younger children, as students move through the junior grades and approach adolescence, they need increasingly more exposure to and instruction in the writing of free-form verse.

The first step in the revision of poetry is to liberate students from the restrictions of rhyme, pattern, and specialty poems. They need to be introduced to the only form of poetry that, at this stage, can approximate and convey the "messy," complex, and near-chaotic content of their exploding consciousness. Free-form verse can help students record and reflect on their perceptions and expand their understanding of their world and themselves.

Even with free-verse, however, students still need to examine how the form of a poem augments and intrinsically enhances its meaning. The heart of the revision process for poetry lies in the student author articulating intentions and comparing those with reader response. In the guidelines that follow, students are asked to reflect on and detail their intentions in creating a specific poem and to predict reader reaction both to the meaning and to the form of the poem. The peer partners are asked to respond in kind, describing what they make of both the meaning and the form of the poem. In the discussion that ensues, the student authors are able to judge precisely what adjustments are necessary to further shape and refine their drafts.

The three models that follow these directions offer a revision sequence for hands-on practice. Please feel free to photocopy or create overhead transparencies for classroom use.

How to use Model 5A: A poetry conference

Direct the class discussion using an overhead transparency of the page. Explain that the left-hand side of the page shows the first draft of a student poem. The right-hand side features the responses of other students during a revision conference, as well as the author's reactions to their questions and comments.

Read aloud the poem and then mention that the student guided the discussion by saying, "The poem sounds O.K., but there's something about it that bothers me and I don't know how to make it better." One by one, address the response comments, emphasizing that these comments were made orally to the author and, that during a revision conference, the author is responsible for making notes on the written work. Using an overhead marker, mark the left-hand side of the page as the student author might have done to note the comments made by the revision partners. (Please see "Teacher Marking Guide," page 74.)

After dealing with the responses, go on to Model 5B.

How to use Model 5B: What to cut?

This page shares the second draft of the poem. The student author was so stimulated by the discussion over the first draft that he wrote a number of new lines in a free-flowing, stream-of-consciousness manner. Photocopy this page and create an overhead transparency. Read aloud from the transparency, then hand out photocopies of the page and assign the activity. The assignment is at the top of the page.

Student Author Guideline on Preparing for a Poetry Peer-revision Conference

Try to measure the success of your poem. Consider why you wrote it and how you hope other people will respond to it and what they will understand about it. Predict the aspects of your poem that your readers will enjoy or be affected or intrigued by.

Before sharing your poem with a peer, establish in your own mind what impact you hope its meaning and form will have on someone else. Decide, as well, how you might direct a conference partner to assist with problematic aspects you have yet to resolve.

Answer any of the following questions that apply to your poem before your first peer conference.

About the **meaning**:

- How do you want readers to respond to this poem?

- What will the poem make them think about?

- What questions or comments will arise?

- What aspects of the meaning, if any, do you think might be unclear or difficult to understand?

About the **form**:

- What aspects of your use of language do you think your readers will appreciate or enjoy?

  Examples:

  — vivid, colorful, apt use of words, phrases, images?

  — effective placement of words, phrases, lines on page?

  — special forms, such as rhyme, optic features, haiku?

Student Guideline for a Peer-revision Partner in a Poetry Revision Conference

After you read the poem aloud several times, try to declare and explain your personal reaction to it. Also, identify those aspects of meaning and form that, for whatever reasons, attracted your attention. First, discuss the poem features you enjoyed or the way the poem affected you. Then, follow up with clarifying questions or helpful suggestions. Any of the following questions that apply to the poem could serve as the basis for your discussion of the poem with the author.

About the **meaning**:

- How did you respond to this poem?

- What did you start thinking about?

- What, if anything, confused you?

- What, if anything, seemed unclear?

- What questions or comments do you have?

About the **form**:

- What aspects of the use of language did you appreciate or enjoy?

  Examples:

  — vivid, colorful, apt use of words, phrases, images?

  — effective placement of words, phrases, lines on page?

  — special forms, such as rhyme, optic features, haiku?

- What constructive suggestions can you offer about the use of language?

  Examples:

  — vivid, colorful, apt use of words, phrases, images?

  — effective placement of words, phrases, lines on page?

  — special forms, such as rhyme, optic features, haiku?

How to use Model 5C: Making choices

The left-hand side of the page features the final draft of the poem and the right-hand side of the page shows the first draft. The assignment is underneath the first draft. Either photocopy this page for use with small groups or create an overhead transparency to use with the whole class. Direct the students to discuss the assigned questions, either as a class group or in smaller groups.

Model 5A: A Poetry Conference

A crippled, autumn-colored cat,
Hobbling, shadow to shadow,
Stiffly through my mind.

Fat and grouchy and, oh, so fine,
When Charlie died,
I lost my innocence.

Response: Why don't you have a title?

Author: I don't know what the title should be.

Response: Maybe you're not sure what you're talking about.

Response: Everything is crippled; the cat and even your thoughts.

Author: I guess I'm feeling sorry for myself and I'm trying not to think about it. I guess it's always in my mind and I'm always pushing it away.

Response: Your thoughts of her keep coming from shadows, along with other thoughts.

Author: When I try to think, my thoughts go into shadows.

Response: What does the line, "I lost my innocence" really mean?

Author: I'm missing something in my life now. It seems I keep losing things I love. I lost my brother, too, and they're linked in my mind. Charlie was always there to cheer me up; things keep dying and going away; there's no comfort any more.

Model 5A: Teacher Marking Guide

title? – what's poem about?

A crippled, autumn-colored (cat,)
Hobbling, shadow to shadow
Stiffly through (my mind.)

– everything crippled
– why?
– thoughts go into shadows

Fat and grouchy and, oh, so fine,
When Charlie died,
(I lost my innocence.)

– missing something
– losing love
– brother ⟷ Charlie
– things dying
– no comfort

Response: Why don't you have a title?

Author: I don't know what the title should be.

Response: Maybe you're not sure what you're talking about.

Response: Everything is crippled; the cat and even your thoughts.

Author: I guess I'm feeling sorry for myself and I'm trying not to think about it. I guess it's always in my mind and I'm always pushing it away.

Response: Your thoughts of her keep coming from shadows, along with other thoughts.

Author: When I try to think, my thoughts go into shadows.

Response: What does the line, "I lost my innocence" really mean?

Author: I'm missing something in my life now. It seems I keep losing things I love. I lost my brother, too, and they're linked in my mind. Charlie was always there to cheer me up; things keep dying and going away; there's no comfort any more.

Model 5B: What to Cut?

The final draft of this poem is 19 lines long. This second draft has more than 60 lines. If you were acting as the author's revision partner, which lines or ideas would you like to see saved? Circle those lines.

Shadowland

losing love
how often can love go
and still return?
losing love is
falling down, deep down
in a dark place, somewhere
a brother, dead
circles of pain
an old woman, cold and lifeless
a brother, so young
a pet companion, gone
shadows on the heart
sad stains from the past
when you lose love
does love survive, ghost-like, still
where does love go,
when a loved one dies,
the love survives, ghost-like
when days become limited
how does love survive
hovering
a restless
    love's ghost survives
the ghost of love
lose and forget

lose and forget
around and around
    flickers and
the sun dims, forever a little,
the sea deepens,
the night grows colder, a
        little alien
while the love survives,
ghost-like
like an orphan
a crippled dream
wandering forever
through a crippled dream.
cruel circles of pain,
    shocks from the past
dark stubborn stains in the mind,
sad reminders
tomorrow
dark shadows on the heart.
    she hobbles
sometimes, see the shape
through the midnight
just beyond that closed door
    down the midnight hallway
a crippled, autumn-colored cat,
    the loss still alive
long dead, but lingering
like a stubborn stain,
a dark shadow on my heart
when the one you love dies
you can feel the shudder

Shadowland

Sometimes, she hobbles
Down the midnight hallway,
A crippled, autumn-colored
cat,
Long dead, but the loss still
alive,
Lingering like a stubborn stain,
A dark shadow on my heart.

When the one you love dies,
The sun dims a little,
The sea deepens,
The night grows colder,
A little more alien,
While, ghost-like, the love
survives,
Wandering forever
Through a crippled dream.

First draft (Shadowland)

A crippled, autumn-colored
cat,
Hobbling, shadow to shadow,
Stiffly through my mind.

Fat and grouchy and, oh, so
fine,
When Charlie died,
I lost my innocence.

Assignment:

1. Compare the two versions. In what ways is the final version an improvement on the first draft?

2. What was lost from the first draft that you wish had been left in? Why?

3. What lines from the second draft (Model 5B) do you wish had been left in? Explain.

Series 6: Revising a Poem 2 (Junior/Intermediate)

> ### Cliché
>
> An expression that has become commonplace and stale through overuse

Experience marks the great divide between adult teachers and youthful writers. A beginning teacher deluged with the overused characters, plots, and expressions found in much student writing is tempted to wonder why today's students aren't more creative and original. An experienced teacher meeting the same metaphors year after year often finds student writing becoming more and more banal as time goes on. Both impressions deny students their right to grow through experience.

For students, an expression such as "cold as ice" remains fresh and vivid and the metaphor "love is a rose" is arresting and evocative. By using the expressions themselves, students imbue their own writing with the impact and emotion they first felt from their initial experience with the language. Expecting students to censor clichéd language before they have personally discovered the limitations of overuse is much like asking students who have never flown to describe the boredom of an overseas flight. They'll get there eventually, but it will take some time and experience. The key in revision is accepting many clichés as genuine and vital forms of expression and using them to unearth in students the links between the heightened language and their own lives.

In student poems, however, the nuggets of expression represented by these clichés, as well as other types of personally significant language, are often buried in a landslide of repetitive and unbroken thoughts and feelings. A useful first step in sifting through this spontaneous outpouring is asking students to identify the expressions and ideas that are absolutely essential to a poem. They might think in terms of the best lines or the ones their readers will enjoy or appreciate most. Students can then be directed to root out unnecessary or ineffective repetition that dulls the impact of those essential expressions and ideas. Finally, they can use spacing to divide a poem into stanzas to further highlight and enhance the various distilled and related lines and images.

The three models that follow offer a revision sequence for hands-on practice. Please feel free to photocopy or create overhead transparencies for classroom use.

How to use Model 6A: Sorting it out

Direct the class discussion using an overhead transparency of the page. The students will also require their own copies for the assigned activities. Explain that the left-hand side of the page shows the first draft of a student poem. The right-hand side features the responses of other students during a revision conference, as well as the author's reactions to their questions and comments.

Read aloud the poem and then mention that the student guided the discussion by saying, "Is there anything I should take out or anything I should add?" One by one, address the response comments, emphasizing that these comments were made orally to the author and, that during a revision conference, the author is responsible for making notes on the written work. Using an overhead marker, mark the left-hand side of the page as the student author might have done to note the comments made by the revision partners. (Please see "Teacher Marking Guide," page 80.) After dealing with the responses, assign the following revision activities:

1. On your copy of the poem, put check marks on the eight ideas or expressions you think the author should keep in the next draft.
2. Next, use this symbol (#) to indicate all the places where you would leave a line to separate the poem into stanzas.
3. On the back of the sheet, write your own ending for the poem.

How to use Model 6B: Discussing options

This page features the second draft of the poem. Photocopy this page and create an overhead transparency. Read aloud from the transparency and then direct the discussion from the questions on the right-hand side of the page. When the discussion is finished, move on to the next model.

How to use Model 6C: Guided revision

The left-hand side of the page presents the first draft of another poem and the right-hand side of the page outlines the assignment based on the poem. Photocopy this page for use with small groups or individuals, and create an overhead transparency to use with the whole class. Read aloud the poem and assign the activities. Either in small groups or as individuals, have the students complete the activities. When the students are finished, ask volunteers to read their versions of the poem and discuss the similarities and differences among them.

My Best Friend

You're always there for me.
When I'm sad, you're sad.
When I'm happy, you're happy.
You know when I need help
And you help me out.
You're the only one who can laugh
And make me feel better.
You always say the right thing at
the right
time.
When I want to talk, you will just
listen.
If I have nothing to say, you talk.
Nobody else can make me laugh so
much.
I love when we share secrets
And even when we're in a fight,
You keep my secrets.
When I'm with my other friends,
I put on a show for them
But I'm still alone.
When I'm with you, I can be myself.
My friendship with you means the
world
to me.
I don't know what I would do
without you.
Our friendship will last forever.
You will always be my best friend.

Response: This is so true. Friends are there for you. Maybe this idea would go better with that of your being helped out.

Response: How do you know your friend is feeling the same way? Maybe they're faking it.

Response: This is true, but you seem to say things over a bit. It's important, but you're repeating all the time. I think I'd leave some of these lines out.

Response: My friend made me laugh so much last week that I had milk coming out of my nose! It was sooo gross!

Response: This part about secrets is so cool! Usually when a friend gets mad they tell all your secrets, like to the whole world and you want to die!

Response: Yeah, that's so real about being alone and being yourself?!

Response: The last four lines are good; I mean they say good things, but it's repeating again. It's like the poem keeps ending over and over. You need to work on this part a bit.

Response: Why not separate some of the ideas in the poem with spaces to keep them from getting too jumbled together?

Model 6A: Teacher Marking Guide

My Best Friend

(handwritten: How do I know?)

You're always there for me.
When I'm sad, you're sad.
When I'm happy, you're happy.
You know when I need help *(handwritten bracket: combine?)*
And you help me out.
You're the only one who can laugh
And make me feel better.
You always say the right thing at
the right
time. *(handwritten: Repeating things?)*
When I want to talk, you will just
listen.
If I have nothing to say, you talk.
Nobody else can make me laugh so
much. ✓
I love when we share secrets *(handwritten: Yes!)*
And even when we're in a fight,
You keep my secrets.
When I'm with my other friends,
I put on a show for them *(handwritten: Yes!)*
But I'm still alone.
When I'm with you, I can be myself.
My friendship with you means the
world
to me.
I don't know what I would do *(handwritten: Repeating?)*
without you.
Our friendship will last forever. *(handwritten: Ending?)*
You will always be my best friend.

(handwritten vertical note left margin: Separate ideas with spaces?)

Response: This is so true. Friends are there for you. Maybe this idea would go better with that of your being helped out.

Response: How do you know your friend is feeling the same way? Maybe they're faking it.

Response: This is true, but you seem to say things over a bit. It's important, but you're repeating all the time. I think I'd leave some of these lines out.

Response: My friend made me laugh so much last week that I had milk coming out of my nose! It was sooo gross!

Response: This part about secrets is so cool! Usually when a friend gets mad they tell all your secrets, like to the whole world and you want to die!

Response: Yeah, that's so real about being alone and being yourself?!

Response: The last four lines are good; I mean they say good things, but it's repeating again. It's like the poem keeps ending over and over. You need to work on this part a bit.

Response: Why not separate some of the ideas in the poem with spaces to keep them from getting too jumbled together?

Model 6B: Discussing Options

My Best Friend

When I'm sad, you get tears in your
eyes.
When I'm happy, you jump up and
down more than I do.

You know when I need help
And you help me out.
You're always there for me.

When I want to talk, you will just
listen.
If I have nothing to say, you always
say the right thing at the right time.
Nobody else can make me laugh so
much.

I love when we share secrets
And even when we're in a fight,
you keep my secrets.

When I'm with my other friends,
I put on a show for them
But I'm still alone.
When I'm with you, I can be myself.

Ending?

Discussion:

1. Were any ideas left out in this version that you think
should have been left in? Were any left in that
should have been left out? Explain the reasons
behind your choices.

2. Were your choices for stanzas different from the
author's? If so, explain why some of your choices
would improve the poem?

3. What important changes in wording did the author
make? Explain why you think these changes did or
did not improve the poem.

4. How did you decide to end the poem? Of all the
endings suggested by your class, what three endings
seem to fit this poem best? What is it about these
endings that makes them so satisfying?

My Teddy Bear

Its fur is soft and ticklish.
Its big brown eyes stare out at
you.
It seems to have a heart and
soul to me.
The leather paws are worn out
and ripped.
There's a rip in the back, too.
The brown nose is like a
chocolate rose bud.
I like to cuddle up beside him
and hold him close and never
let him go.
When I feel lonely or sad, I
always hold him close.
When I'm with him, I feel happy.
When I'm afraid or worried, I
feel better.
I don't tell people about him
because they'd make fun of me.
Even my friends can be cruel.
But he has comforted me time
and time again and that's why
he's my favorite teddy bear!!

Revision activities:

1. Put check marks on the ideas you would keep in the next draft.

2. Indicate where you would divide the poem into stanzas.

3. What important changes in wording would you suggest to make some of the ideas more vivid or specific?

4. How would you change the order of some of the ideas or switch some of the lines around?

5. Write your version of the next draft of this poem.

Series 7: Revising a Prose Narrative into a Poem (Intermediate)

As demonstrated in the previous series of models, peer-revision conferences allow students to become more independent, self-reliant, and empowered within the drafting process. Collaboration among students develops spontaneously as they take control of their own writing, have something to say, and require assistance to say it effectively. In this regard, peer revision becomes a true problem-solving activity.

The interactions during conferences can generate and test ideas in unpredictable and intriguing ways. In this series of revision models, students witness the empowering possibilities of collaboration as the peer partners struggle to make the form of the prose narrative in question fit its content. As they respond to the writing and gradually think through the revisions, the students demonstrate the recursive and functional nature of drafting.

The four models that follow these directions offer a revision sequence for hands-on practice. Please feel free to photocopy or create overhead transparencies for classroom use.

How to use Model 7A: Finding the right form

Direct the class discussion using an overhead transparency of the page. Explain that the left-hand side of the page shows the first draft of a student narrative. The right-hand side notes the responses of other students during a revision conference. Although the first-draft narrative contains a variety of spelling and usage errors, since the students were focusing on revision, most of these errors were ignored. The errors were addressed only if they obscured the meaning.

Read aloud the narrative and mention that the student author tried to guide the peer conference by saying, "I think I've got a lot of good description here, but does it all make sense?" One by one, address the response comments, emphasizing that these comments were made orally to the author and, that during a revision conference, the author is responsible for making notes on the written work. Using an overhead marker, mark the left-hand side of the page as the student author might have done to note the comments made by the revision partners. (Please see "Teacher Marking Guide," page 86.)

After dealing with the original responses, invite other revision suggestions from the class. Note these additional responses on the page. Explain then that the author took the first draft and turned it into a poem as suggested. Ask the students to make their own first-draft poems based on the narrative and the student responses.

How to use Model 7B: Comparing choices

The left-hand side of the page features the first draft of the poem developed from Model 7A. Create an overhead transparency for use with the whole class or photocopy the poem for small-group discussions. Directions for the discussion appear on the right-hand side of the page.

How to use Model 7C: Inviting changes

The left-hand side of the page shows the second draft of the poem and the student responses. Direct the class discussion using an overhead transparency of the page. After dealing with the original responses and marking reminders on the poem, invite the class to make other revision suggestions based on their revision conferences on this draft. Note these additional responses on the page.

How to use Model 7D: Evaluating the process

The left-hand side of the page features the final draft of the poem and some comments about the end of the process. The right-hand side of the page contains the original narrative and directions for the activities based on both the poem and the narrative. Create an overhead transparency and photocopy the poem. After the students, in revision pairs or small groups, complete the activities suggested on the photocopied pages, take up the exercise with the class group on the overhead transparency and survey the students for the grading of each piece.

On the Beach

On the beach were life is a holiday and games are played. The sun's brilliance, gleaming on the white, crystal sand. The girls hair is as blond as the sand.

People watch the water roll in and making ripples, and shifting the sand. As the sun falls and the moon rises, the stars can be seeing.

The party's start and never end, and love is made on the sands.

Response: Maybe the title could tell more about what's happening on the beach or what the story is really about.

Response: I like the words and things in the first paragraph, but the sentences don't make sense.

Response: I like how you have the sun and the sand and the girl's hair all the same.

Response: You've got a whole bunch of nice word pictures, but it doesn't seem like a story. Nothing happens. It's more like you're describing a picture or something.

Response: Why not make it a poem? You could take out all the images and arrange them on lines.

Response: How can the stars be "seeing"? Maybe you mean "seen"? What about a more descriptive word like "shone" or "twinkled"?

Response: The ending's kind of rude and it seems sort of added on.

Other responses:

Model 7A: Teacher Marking Guide

On the Beach

what's happening? *what's story about?*

On the beach were life is a holiday and games are played. The sun's brilliance, gleaming on the white, crystal sand. The girls hair is as blond as the sand.

– check sentence

People watch the water roll in and making ripples, and shifting the sand. As the sun falls and the moon rises, the stars can be ~~seeing~~. *seen → twinkled? shone?*

– picture? – poem?

The party's start and never end, and love is made on the sands.

– ending?

Response: Maybe the title could tell more about what's happening on the beach or what the story is really about.

Response: I like the words and things in the first paragraph, but the sentences don't make sense.

Response: I like how you have the sun and the sand and the girl's hair all the same.

Response: You've got a whole bunch of nice word pictures, but it doesn't seem like a story. Nothing happens. It's more like you're describing a picture or something.

Response: Why not make it a poem? You could take out all the images and arrange them on lines.

Response: How can the stars be "seeing"? Maybe you mean "seen"? What about a more descriptive word like "shone" or "twinkled"?

Response: The ending's kind of rude and it seems sort of added on.

Other responses:

Model 7B: Comparing Choices

Directions: Compare your version of the poem with the model at left. What comments or suggestions would you offer the author?

Endless Beach?
Summer on the Beach?
Endless Summer?
On the Beach?

Responses:

On the beach
life is a holiday
and games are played.

Bodies on the beach
Catching a few rays.
The golden sun gleams
brilliantly on the white, crystal
sand.
And The girls hair as blond as
the sand.

People watch the water roll in
making ripples, and shifting
the sand.
As the sun falls, and the
moon rises,
and the stars shine like silver,
The party's start
And never end
and love is made on the sands.

Endless Summer

On the beach,
games are played
and life is a holiday.

The sun gleams brilliantly
on the white, crystal sand and
the girl's blond hair,
as she catches a few rays.

The water rolls in
making ripples and
shifting the sand.

The sun falls,
the moon rises,
the stars shine like silver.

The parties start
and never end
and love is made on the sands.

Response: Why is the summer endless?

Response: These lines don't sound like the rest of the poem. They don't tell you a lot or describe anything.

Response: I really like the descriptive language, but who's the girl? Is anybody else on the beach?

Response: I can picture the scenes clearly in both these stanzas. What about using some more description, like "restless water" or "golden sand"?

Response: This stanza doesn't seem to have the same feeling as the others. It doesn't seem to fit. It's like it's in a different world and you're trying to shock people with it. What about a different ending?

Other responses:

Model 7D: Evaluating the Process

Comment: At some point in the revision process, the author is satisfied or can't think of anything else to say or runs out of time or just gets tired of the piece. For whatever reason, the piece is finished and handed in for marking. The changes from the last draft are highlighted.

Directions: Now compare the final version of the poem with the original descriptive narrative. <u>Underline</u> the words and phrases from the original that appear in the final draft of the poem. If you were grading these pieces on a scale of 1–10, what mark would you give "Endless Summer" and what mark would you give "On the Beach"?

Endless Summer

Down on the beach,
It's like a picture postcard
That never changes.

The noonday sun is brilliant,
Gleaming on the white, crystal sand,
Toasting the sunbathers
With laser-like rays.

The restless water rolls in
making carefree ripples
And shifting the golden sand.

As the fading sun falls,
The pale moon rises
And the diamond stars shine.

Day turns to night,
Night turns to day,
And the summer goes on and on.

On the Beach

On the beach were life is a holiday and games are played. The sun's brilliance, gleaming on the white, crystal sand. The girls hairs is as blond as the sand.

People watch the water roll in and making ripples, and shifting the sand. As the sun falls and the moon rises, the stars can be seeing.

The party's start and never end, and love is made on the sands.

Series 8: Revising a Project (Junior/Intermediate)

> ### Project
>
> An extended school assignment, such as a research investigation, a formal experiment, or an elaborate collection

Long before the students ever see the assignment, the classroom teacher has a lot to do with how well a project will be revised. In some ways similar to an essay, a project takes its shape from the set of explanations, instructions, and requirements that establish what needs to be done and in what manner. With precise, comprehensive, and easy-to-understand directions, students have a concrete basis on which to judge and revise the content and expression of their project. If the students know before they ever begin the project how they will be evaluated, moreover, the summative evaluation of the projects can have an important formative outcome. If students know precisely the criteria by which they will be evaluated, they will more readily direct their efforts to meeting those criteria and will use them when revising their material. When students are ready to revise their projects, advise them to follow "Student Guideline for Revising a Project" (next page).

The four models that follow these directions offer a revision sequence for hands-on practice. Please feel free to photocopy or create overhead transparencies for classroom use.

How to use Model 8A: Understanding the assignment

Using an overhead transparency of the page, review the mathematics assignment, "The Cube Building," and the evaluation criteria. You may wish to refer to this material again as the revision conference unfolds.

How to use Model 8B: Testing the first draft

Direct the class discussion using an overhead transparency of the page. Explain that the left-hand side of the page shows the first draft of the student project. The right-hand side features the responses of other students during a revision conference. Although the first-draft essay contains a variety of spelling and usage errors, since the students were focusing on revision, most of these errors were ignored. The errors were addressed only if they obscured the meaning.

Read aloud the project and, one by one, address the response comments, emphasizing that these comments were made orally to the author and that during a revision conference the author is responsible for making notes on the written work. Using an overhead marker, mark the left-hand side of the page as the student author might have done to note the comments made by the revision partners. (Please see "Teacher Marking Guide," page 95.) After dealing with the original responses, review the assignment instructions and invite other revision suggestions from the class. Note these additional responses on the page.

Student Guideline for Revising a Project

As you revise your project, keep the following questions in mind:

• Did you do what you were asked to do in the way you were asked to do it?

• Are any sections of your project confusing, awkwardly worded, or incomplete?

Take the following steps as you revise:

1. Go back to your original instructions. Check off each requirement on your finished project. If any elements are missing or are only partially realized, you must complete them fully.

2. Go back to the evaluation criteria. Check off each component as it appears in your project. Self-evaluate how well you've met each criterion and assign yourself a mark. Revise each component you find unsatisfactory.

3. Check the way you've expressed your ideas. If any sections are confusing, awkwardly worded, or repetitive, revise them.

4. Ask someone to read your project aloud. Does it sound the way you thought it would? If not, focus on the unsatisfactory aspects in your revision. Ask someone also to check other aspects of your project, such as computations, the accuracy of drawings or models, or the general appearance. If some elements are inaccurate or not creating your desired impression, make any necessary changes.

How to use Model 8C: Evaluating results

The left-hand side of the page features the next draft of the report from Model 8B. Photocopy the page. Call for students to conduct discussion in revision pairs or in small groups. The students will again need to review the assignment. Instruct them first to evaluate the project according to the marking scheme, leaving out the section called Appearance. Once they've decided what the other sections are worth, ask for further responses to guide additional revisions, keeping in mind what they've learned through the marking exercise.

How to use Model 8D: What would you suggest?

The left-hand side of the page shows another student-written report generated by the same assignment. Either photocopy this page or create an overhead transparency. Direct the students, either as a class group or in smaller groups, to conduct a revision conference. If the conference is conducted with the aid of an overhead transparency, act as surrogate author and mark the essay in response to the revision comments and suggestions. If smaller groups are used, designate a student from each group as scribe.

Model 8A: Understanding the Assignment

The Cube Building

What you do:

- Design a building using four cubes.
- Draw your building on large, dotted paper.
- Figure out how much your building will cost (see below).
- Write a final report (see below).

What you draw:

- Make a large drawing of your building.
- Use color and include windows and other details.
- Include scenery, grass, trees, water, and anything else you think might be interesting and appealing.

What's in the final report:

- Four paragraphs:
  1. A name for the building and a description of it
  2. Reasons for the design:
     - Why did you make this shape?
     - Was it cheap or expensive?
     - How did you want it to look?
  3. Building cost: (See top of right column.)
  4. Tell what you thought of the project. Begin by noting what you liked about it. Feel free to speak your mind and say what you didn't like and why.

What it costs:

- Figure out the cost according to this plan:
  - 1st floor - $100
  - 2nd floor - $200
  - 3rd floor - $300
  - 4th floor - $500
- The land under any cube costs $100.
- Any square that can be rained on will cost $100.

How the project is marked:

- Appearance: /10
  - effort includes color, neatness
  - all sections complete

- Description: /10
  - described fully, named, and a reason for the name

- Reasoning: /10
  - all questions explained

- Cost: /10
  - accurate and fully explained

- Conclusion: /10
  - detailed and complete

- Expression: /10
  - clear, correct, and vivid language

My Project

my building is the great marriott hotel I named it that because my last name is marriott and i've heard of the marriott hotel so I chose to use that for my building name. the number of cubes on each floor are two. I picked this building shape because I thought it would take up alot of space so it would cost a lot of money and because it looked pretty neat. My total is $600 for everything. Conclusions: I liked how my building cost alot of money I thought it was quite interesting to figure this out. I liked how I got to do something a bit fun for a change in math. I think the building was nice and it had a nice setting.

Response: Why not use a better title like "The Great Marriott Hotel"?

Response: This is a good reason but you could shorten it a bit.

Response: The instructions said to describe your building. Can you add more details?

Response: Why did you want it to cost a lot of money?

Other responses:

Model 8B: Teacher Marking Guide

Great Marriott Hotel?

My Project

my building is the great marriott hotel I named it that *[shorten?]* because my last name is marriott *+?* and i've heard of the marriot hotel so I chose to use that for my building name. the number of cubes

✱ more details / describe /

on each floor are two. I picked this building shape because I thought it would take up alot of space so it would *[why?]* cost a lot of money and because it looked pretty neat. My total is $600 for everything. Conclusions: I liked how my building cost alot of money I thought it was quite interesting to figure this out. I liked how I got to do something a bit fun for a change in math. I think the building was nice and it had a nice setting.

Response: Why not use a better title like "The Great Marriott Hotel"?

Response: This is a good reason but you could shorten it a bit.

Response: The instructions said to describe your building. Can you add more details?

Response: Why did you want it to cost a lot of money?

Other responses:

The Great Marriott Hotel

My name is Marriott and I've heard of the marriott hotel and that's what I called my building. I used two red cubes beside each other and two on top of them. The top cube has a big gold M on it and the bottom cube has big gold doors. The hotel has gold curtains on all the windows and a swimming pool on the roof. I wanted to rent to rich people so I made it cost alot. The cost was $100 for the first floor and $200 for the second floor and $200 for the land and $200 for the rained on part. The total was $700 for everything.

I liked how my building cost alot of money and I thought it was quite interesting to figure this out. I like how I got to do something a bit fun for a change in math. I didn't understand some things like I wasn't sure if I was supposed to pay money for the pool on the roof. I thought my building turned out nice.

Evaluation:

- Appearance: /10
  - effort includes color, neatness
  - all sections complete

- Description: /10
  - described fully, named, and a reason for the name

- Reasoning: /10
  - all questions explained

- Cost: /10
  - accurate and fully explained

- Conclusion: /10
  - detailed and complete

- Expression: /10
  - clear, correct, and vivid language

Responses:

Model 8D: What Would You Suggest?

The Cube Building

Responses:

My building has 2 levels with two cubes on each level. My building is named the Elite Complex Building. The building of this building costs $1000. I chose this perticular area becaus it looks nice.

I chose to build this shape because it costs the less where this building costs $1000 the other cost up to $1200 or more. I wanted to save some cash for it to have good surroundings. if it was in the country it would look ugly.

My building cost $1000 this is how I came to this cost. First level = $100. 2nd level = $200. Land = $100. roof = $100.

I think this was a great idea because it would help us to use money in good ways when we're old. When this project was assigned I thought it was due monday and I started panicking because it was Friday and I for got my math duotang. On monday things worked out allright.

CHAPTER 5

An Editing Toolkit

Self- and Peer-editing

Collaboration in the editing/proofreading cycle is indispensable. While students will detect a few obvious errors in their own drafts, in most cases, if they knew the correct convention, they would use it. They need to actively combine forces in peer-editing conferences to pool their personal knowledge, experiences, and resources to bring their drafts into a camera-ready state. Besides, authors at any age tend to read what they think they've written rather than what they've actually written. A fresh pair of eyes helps to cast a revealing light onto the text. The more students struggle with language conventions, moreover, the more peer conferences they may need.

In the self-editing stage, however, one aspect of standard usage can be effectively managed — spelling, an essential communication skill. The misspelling of a word not only creates an obstacle to understanding, but also often leaves a negative impression of the writer's abilities. The spell-check feature of word-processing programs, therefore, can provide valuable help to a student writer. Using spell check must be an absolutely inviolable component of the editing process.

Even with spell check, however, collaboration at the keyboard is essential. Presented by the computer with a list of alternatives to a questionable spelling, students will often recognize the correct form. As such, spell check operates as an external mnemonic aid. When students don't recognize the correct choice, instead of guessing, they should engage a nearby peer in a brief, ad hoc conference. Simply asking "What's the right one?" can clear up the confusion and reinforce for the writer the image of the correct spelling for the next time the word comes up.

Students, by and large, are more confident about what they're supposed to do in peer-editing conferences than in peer-revision conferences. They understand that they're supposed to look for mistakes. Not surprisingly, they tend to focus on the spellings of words. While they know they're supposed to be looking at grammar and usage, as well, they tend to scrutinize the text for more concrete practices, such as the use of quotation marks or end punctuation.

Either in the self-editing stage or in peer-editing conferences, simple, straightforward checklists can serve as invaluable references and resources. The photocopiable checklists in this chapter are meant to correct, simplify, clarify, and invigorate the use of language and support students as they go about the often daunting task of editing their writing before the teacher marks it. The selected items, however, are far from exhaustive; too many examples tend to overwhelm and confuse. For older students, specific sections can be augmented by any standard text. Student checklists cover editing symbols, usage do's and don't's, titles, punctuation, and easily confused words. See "Editing Symbols Checklist," on page 101, to get students started on marking up their own or others' writing.

At this stage in the drafting process, students will find the checklists from Chapter 3, covering paragraphs (page 35), sentences (pages 36–37), and word choices (page 39), both pertinent and useful. Checklists can be placed in students' writing folders for easy reference.

Is It Grammar or Is It Usage ?

Grammar

A study of the patterns of word formation in a language and the structure of word order in sentences, clauses, and phrases

Usage

The customary or preferred way of using specific items of language in such areas as pronunciation, vocabulary, and syntax

Grammar refers to the system of rules that govern language; usage refers to specific items of language use rather than the entire system. The study of usage pertains to examining the choices people make in using language and determining the acceptability of those choices. The editing process, therefore, focuses primarily on questions of usage rather than grammar.

The concept of making choices is key to a positive approach to editing. Usage varies according to the situation. Expressions acceptable in speech may be unacceptable in writing. Usages appropriate for informal, personal exchanges may be inappropriate in more formal settings. As students are helped to make appropriate choices, they begin to discard the punitive dichotomy of correct and incorrect in favor of trying to make the best choices possible to enhance the meaning they intend.

Editing Symbols Checklist

When editing, people automatically strike out an unwanted word or phrase with a horizontal line. Other editing symbols indicate a range of mistakes to correct or improvements to make. Some symbols, such as $\underline{Sp}$ for spelling error, are already in common use. As you edit your writing, the following symbols should help you mark changes in a fast and efficient manner.

⊙   Insert period.

       Example: I finished the assignment⊙

≡   Use capital (upper case) letters for the letters underlined.

       Example: lake of the woods

∧   Insert letter, word, phrase, or punctuation mark.

       Example: How are you?

Leave more space.

       Example: pioneer#life

¶   Begin a new paragraph.

       Example: "Yes," she said. ¶ "No," he said.

$\underline{Sp}$ Correct the spelling.

       Example: Thier books fell on the floor.
           $\overline{Sp}$

Usage Do's and Don't's Checklist

If you see or hear the same usage error often enough, you're apt to start believing that the usage is actually correct. Teachers fall into this trap time and again when correcting or editing their students' work. That dictionary on your teacher's desk is well-thumbed. Certain errors are repeated so often in casual conversation that many people become hopelessly confused about what is or is not acceptable practice. While standard usage changes over time, some types of common errors remain unacceptable. Since other people often form impressions of us from how we use language, becoming aware of and getting rid of these kinds of mistakes is essential. The following list of do's and don't's should help.

- *Do* use **anywhere**.
  Example: The bus doesn't stop **anywhere** near here.
  Don't use anywheres or anyplace.

- *Do* use **try to come**.
  Example: **Try to come** early to the party.
  Don't use try and come.

- *Do* use **a long way**.
  Example: I live **a long way** from here.
  Don't use a long ways.

- *Do* use **both**.
  Example: The teacher gave a pencil to **both** of them.
  Don't use the both.

- *Do* use **first, second, third**, etc.
  Example: **First**, we'll clean up the kitchen; **second**, we'll do the laundry; and, **third**, we'll clean out the basement.
  Don't use firstly, secondly, thirdly, etc.

- *Do* use **1st, 2nd, 3rd**, etc.
  Example: The Math team has games on the **1st, 2nd**, and **3rd** of May.
  Don't use 1st., 2nd., 3rd., etc.

- *Do* use periods after the abbreviations **Mrs. and Mr.**
  Example: **Mr.** and **Mrs.** Brown came to the party.
  Don't use periods after Miss or Ms; they aren't abbreviations.

- *Do* use the expression **a lot**.
  Example: I have **a lot** of work to do.
  Don't use alot. The two words are always separated.

- *Do* use **very**.
  Example: I'm **very** mad at her.
  Don't use good and. Example: I'm good and mad at her.

- *Do* use **fewer** when referring to something you can count.
  Example: If I make **fewer** than three mistakes on the test, I'll be happy.
  Don't use less. Less refers to something you can measure.

- *Do* use **less** when referring to something you can measure.
  Example: I think I'll put **less** flour in the recipe next time.

- *Do* use **lie** when you mean place a body in a flat position on a surface.
  Example: **Lie** down when you're tired.
  Don't use lay. Lay means place or set down in a particular position.

- *Do* use **lay** when you mean place or set down in a particular position.
  Example: **Lay** your book on the table.

To Capitalize or Not to Capitalize Checklist

Some uses for capital letters seem more straightforward than others. Most people, for example, realize that the first word of a sentence is always capitalized or that proper names, such as Canada or Martin Luther King, always begin with a capital letter. In other situations, deciding when to capitalize or when not to capitalize can be confusing. Check your next draft for the following examples:

- Days, months, holidays, and holy days are capitalized.
  Examples: Monday, June, Thanksgiving Day, Yom Kippur

- Adjectives formed from proper names are capitalized, but the words they modify are not.
  Examples: Canadian lakes, Muslim customs

- The beginning of dialogue, set with quotation marks, should be capitalized.
  Example: My father yelled, "Take out the trash immediately."

- The names of the seasons are not capitalized.
  Example: I like to walk in the woods in the fall.

- The points of the compass are not capitalized when they indicate direction, but they are usually capitalized when they refer to a geographic region.
  Examples: The lake is south of the main highway.
  I was born in the South, but moved to the North at an early age.

- School subjects are not capitalized unless they are the names of languages.
  Example: I'm doing well in French, history, and science.

- Words showing family relationships are not capitalized unless they are used with a person's name or in place of a person's name.
  Examples: My mother and father really like Uncle Bill and Aunt Dorothy.
  "What did you say, Dad? I was listening to Uncle Bill."

Titles Checklist

Capitalization is just one of the conventions governing the writing of titles.

- Use capital (upper case) letters for the first, last, and all other important words in a title.

- Words, such as *a*, *an*, and *the*, and short connecting words, such as *and* and *with*, are usually considered not important enough to be capitalized.

- Remember to capitalize all verbs, even the short ones, such as *is* or *be*.

- In handwritten reports, underline the titles of books, magazines, newspapers, and radio and television programs.

- With reports done on a word processor, titles are often highlighted in a bold or an italicized face instead of underlined. Underlining is still correct.

- Use double quotation marks for the title of a poem, song, story, or newspaper or magazine article.

Pursuing Clarity

Punctuation

The use of approved, specific marks other than letters to help clarify the meaning in something written

---

Punctuation forms part of the palette writers have available to get their meanings across to readers. Writers control the use of punctuation; they make choices about punctuation for the same reason they make word choices: for understanding. Advise student writers to think of punctuation from the point of view of someone reading aloud whatever they've written. What signposts give them the direction they need to pause, raise or lower the voice, or inflect the voice to mark a question or exclamation? A writer erects these signposts whenever they're needed to assist someone else to make sense of what otherwise would be a jumble of words. Punctuation helps the reader understand how the writing should sound and clarifies what it means.

Although some usage may vary in style, the following guidelines (pages 107–13) illustrate some of the more conventional uses of terminal punctuation, commas, colons, semicolons, quotation marks, hyphens, and apostrophes.

Word choices also directly affect understanding. Even though student writers might make effective word choices, they often inadvertently confuse words they've selected with words that sound or look similar. For those students who frequently confuse certain words, a checklist in their writing folders serves as a handy and effective editing tool. You may find these photocopiable resources useful: "Checklist of Words Easily Confused" and "Checklist of Words Easily Confused That Are Homonyms" (pages 114–16).

Punctuation Guidelines
Part 1: Terminal Punctuation, Commas, Colons, Semicolons

Without punctuation, your writing would be incomprehensible to anyone else. These signposts help your readers understand your specific intentions. Punctuation directs how the writing should sound and clarifies what it means. The following definitions and examples illustrate some conventional uses of punctuation. Use them to guide your self-editing and peer-editing conferences.

Terminal punctuation

Period
The sign that signifies the full pause at the end of a declarative sentence. A period also highlights the use of an abbreviation.

- A period indicates that a sentence has ended.

  The sentence came to a full stop.

- A period also indicates the use of most abbreviations. Note, however, that metric abbreviations do not use periods.

  Alta. (Alberta)
  Sept. (September)
  m.p.h. (miles per hour)
  km (kilometre)

Question mark
The punctuation mark used at the end of a sentence to indicate that the sentence is a question

- A question mark indicates a question.

  What did you mean by that?
  You lost your lunch money?

Exclamation mark

The punctuation mark used after a word, phrase, or sentence to provide emphasis

- An exclamation mark indicates emphasis. (Use it sparingly. Overuse weakens the intended emphasis.)

> Fire! Fire! Please help me!
> What a ridiculous thing to say!

Commas

Commas

The written equivalents of the pauses in everyday speech that break sentences or divide a word series to clarify and prevent ambiguity in meaning

- Commas separate expressions of time or manner at the beginning of a sentence if the absence of a comma would confuse the reader.

> Shortly after, the test began.
> Without warning, the horse swerved.

- Commas separate words, phrases, or clauses in a series. Two different conventions are commonly used (please see examples). Choose one style and be consistent.

Alternative 1:
> He checked his binder for a pencil, paper and pen.
> She rollerbladed across the road, down the sidewalk and up the driveway.

Alternative 2:
> He checked his binder for a pencil, paper, and pen.
> She rollerbladed across the road, down the sidewalk, and up the driveway.

- A comma separates the principal, or main, statement in a sentence from a dependent or conditional statement.

Correct:
> When the bell rang, the class stampeded for the door.
> If I had the time, I would go to the game.

Also correct:
   The class stampeded for the door when the bell rang.
   I would go to the game if I had the time.

- A comma is used after the salutation (beginning greeting) of a personal letter.

   Dear Ms Thibeau,

- A comma is used to mark off the name of a person spoken to in direct speech. (In the second example, two commas are necessary.)

   Let's hurry, Frank.
   We must leave right away, Frank, or we'll be late.
   Frank, we must leave now!

- Two commas separate the names in addresses and places, set off words and phrases in apposition, and indicate interjections.

   She was born in Calgary, Alberta, in 1960.
   Mrs. Shaw, the gym teacher, coached the volleyball team.
   Punctuality, of course, is a necessity in any school.

Colons

> ### Colons
>
> These punctuation marks are used to separate the main part of a sentence from an explanation, example, quotation, or list; they are also used after the salutation of a business letter, in certain numerical expressions, and between titles and subtitles in books

Examples:

We knew now why she was smiling: she had won the game.

Please send the following supplies: a warm blanket, hiking boots, spare socks, canned food, and chocolate bars.

To whom it may concern:

The class ended at 12:45 p.m.

Learning to Punctuate: The Colon

Semicolons

Semicolons

These punctuation marks are sometimes used to join two independent, but related statements; they also separate items in a series that already contain punctuation.

Examples:

I like baseball; however, I never watch it on television.

The goals were scored by Sean Day, Gr. 7, Ms Maharaj's class; Thierry Henry, Gr. 8, Mr. Faber's class; and Gerald Chan, Gr. 8, Ms Thurston's class.

Punctuation Guidelines
Part 2: Quotation Marks, Hyphens, Apostrophes

Quotation marks

Quotation marks

These marks are used to indicate the beginning and end of a directly quoted passage or to enclose a word or phrase used in an unusual way.

- Quotation marks enclose the actual words spoken.

  "Begin now," the teacher said.

- If the end of the sentence is also the end of the directly quoted passage, a period is put inside the quotation mark.

  The teacher said, "Begin now."

- When the sentence doesn't directly quote the speaker, quotation marks are not used. The word *that* often indicates such an indirect quote.

  The teacher said that we should begin now.

- Whether or not a question mark or exclamation mark is placed inside or outside the quotation marks depends on the sense or meaning of the sentence.

  Did he say, "I'm finished"?
  He said, "Are you finished?"

- Single quotation marks indicate a quote within a quote.

  "When I asked him to the movies," she said, "he replied, 'Of course, I'll go with you.'"

- Quotation marks indicate the use of an unusual word for the writer or in that particular context.

  The whole evening turned out to be a "bummer."

Hyphens

- Hyphens are used to indicate that part of a word is carried over to the next line. With word processors, however, this function is no longer necessary. If a word is divided, the division occurs between syllables.

   During his warmup, the pitcher had difficulty throw-
   ing the ball over the plate.

- Hyphens are used to join the segments of some compound words.

   mother-in-law

- Hyphens are used when writing fractions.

   two-thirds or four-sixths

- A hyphen replaces *and* in such old numerical forms as *forty and eight*.

   forty-eight or four thousand, forty-eight

- A hyphen creates a compound of a number and an adjective.

   She rode her new two-wheeled bicycle.
   The advertising agency created a three-pronged ad campaign.

- A hyphen connects two or more adjectives preceding a noun.

   She wore a dark-green blouse.
   He got caught in stop-and-go traffic.

   (Note that no hyphen is used after a noun or with an adverb ending in -*ly*.)

   The blouse she was wearing was dark green.
   He tried to keep up with the swiftly moving traffic.

Apostrophes

Apostrophes
Apostrophes show omissions, possession, or the plural of words that have no plural of their own.

- An apostrophe indicates a letter or letters missing in contractions.

  I can't go out tonight. (can not = can't)
  It's late. (It is = It's)
  They're never on time. (They are = They're)

- An apostrophe indicates a possessive; in this example, a single student.

  the student's books

- An apostrophe indicates a possessive; in this example, more than one student.

  the students' books

- An apostrophe indicates a possessive; in this example, more than one child, but the plural does not end in *s*.

  the children's books

- The apostrophe is placed after the last word when a group of words takes the possessive.

  somebody else's pencil

- Some possessives do *not* use an apostrophe.

  hers, ours, yours, theirs

- *Whose* is the possessive; *who's* is the contraction for *who is*.

  Whose book is that?

- An apostrophe indicates the plural of letters, numbers, or words that have no plural of their own.

  How many a's are in aardvark?
  The winning lottery number contained three 8's.
  You have too many and's in your sentence.

Checklist of Words Easily Confused

Some words are so similar in the way they sound or the way they look that they are easily confused. Some of the more common examples are used in phrases that illustrate their differences and are listed below. Following the list is a section for you to add some other words that you often confuse.

accept a gift / everyone came **except** for John

breath of fresh air / **breathe** deeply

speak to a friend / make a **speech**

clothes that you wear / **cloths** that you clean with

they **were** so tired that / **where** they live / **we're** here (we are)

a **loose** button / will **lose** the button

a **quiet** room / **quite** a big noise

faster **than** lightning / not until **then**

Personal additions

Checklist of Words Easily Confused That Are Homonyms

Homonyms are even more easily confused than the sort of words listed in the previous checklist because they sound almost exactly the same.

Homonym

A word with the same oral or written form as another word. The term *homonym* covers both homophones and homographs.

Homophone

A word with the same pronunciation as another word, regardless of spelling

Homograph

One of two or more words that share the same spelling but differ in meaning and pronunciation

---

Homonyms are spell-check resistant; if words are spelled correctly, the computer accepts them. Homographs usually aren't a problem. Since we pronounce the words differently, we know whether we mean to *row* a boat or to have a *row* with another person. Homophones are another matter. Since these homonyms crop up many times, personal inspection must do what the computer can't. The homophones in the following reference checklist are commonly misused. When you spot them in your own writing, come back to these examples as needed.

they're   their   there

First, notice that the first three letters of all three words are **t h e**.
Notice now the difference in the way they are used:

They're can only be used to replace **they are**.
Their is a possessive, as in **their** books or **their** clothes.
There is used in **there is** and **there are** or when referring to a place, as in "She went **there** for a rest."

who's   whose

Who's can only be used to replace **who is.**
Whose is a possessive, as in **whose books** or **whose clothes**.

your   you're

You're can only be used to replace **you are**.
Your is a possessive, as in **your** bike or **your** house.

it's   its

It's can only be used to replace **it is**. Any other time, use **its**.

Personal additions

Duty or Donkey Work?

Why do teachers in all subject areas spend so much of their valuable time on the donkey work of editing their students' writing? Marking pens in hand, day after day, they meticulously hunt through class set after class set of notes or composition after composition, tracking down every spelling mistake, punctuation error, or usage and grammar lapse. Like a circular nightmare, the task never ends. Yet generation after generation of teachers continues the time-honored and time-consuming task unabated, and no one questions why.

At one time, the way teachers themselves were supervised and evaluated affected how they taught and evaluated their own students. For example, school principals and district inspectors expected all teachers to do much the same thing in the same way and at the same time throughout a school and a school district. All teachers were issued the same texts across a grade level and across the curriculum and were required to work through them at a similar pace. Student notebooks could then be checked for evidence that teachers were progressing through their textbooks in the prescribed and systematic manner. A wise teacher ensured that every piece of written work students produced was titled, with the title underlined, and dated to facilitate their own evaluation. Pagination and a complete table of contents, of course, was *de rigueur* for each and every notebook. Notebooks and compositions, cross-hatched in red corrections, moreover, offered further evidence of a dedicated and hard-working professional; an untouched page suggested that a teacher was negligent. When notebooks came home, parents and guardians also assumed that a "colorful" confirmation of a teacher's tireless supervision and direction would be present. Not surprisingly, if a page of student notes was, indeed, error-free, teachers made sure they initialed the page as proof to parents and supervisors alike that they were productive and dutiful. The expression that "evaluation is the tail that wags the dog" is commonplace today; in the past, some other dog's tail was wagging your dog.

But that was then and this is now. What about today?

Except in the case of work made public, such as the publishing of compositions, notes and draft material don't need to be "camera-ready." Unless something about the correction process intrinsically benefits students, a perfect draft is unnecessary. However, all too often, an adult indicates the surface errors in a student's writing and the student corrects those errors.

Given the time they spend on doing it, teachers, in fact, must believe that a close marking of surface errors is one of the most potent learning/teaching strategies yet devised. While unsupported by any kind of research or evidence, common wisdom says that unless students correct these mistakes, they will keep making them. Common wisdom also suggests that unless students are forced to focus on the correct language, they will never learn conventional usage. It reflects a belief that students are lazy and that undergoing this repetitive, mindless process of correction is enough to keep them from making the same errors again. For these reasons, common wisdom has kept teachers chained to their marking pens for generations, acting as tireless, unpaid editors and proofreaders.

If teachers truly believed in this practice, they wouldn't get so frustrated as students *do* make the same mistakes or create new errors while correcting the errors pointed out to them. Far from developing in students the motivation, confidence, skills, and practice required to shape and monitor their own writing, this practice operates in an inimical fashion, discouraging risk taking, encouraging a warped view of the writing process, and stunting growth in writing skills. With all that practice, however, teachers are certainly honing their own editing/proofreading skills and, if the truth were known, still providing concrete proof to parents and supervisors alike that they are actively on the job.

Perhaps it's time to put the responsibility for editing back where it belongs — on the person who does the writing.

Preparing and Presenting the Feast

Knowing when *not* to draft is as important a skill as first learning how to draft. Consider the purpose of the writing. Language is for thinking as well as for communicating. Writing and thinking are so closely linked that many kinds of journal writing, for example, are pursued for the sake of reflection and inner growth alone. In these cases, applying the revising/editing cycle of the writing process would be counterproductive. If fluency were insisted upon, the informal, everyday, repetitive, and recursive language of personal thought would dry up. So, too, would the problem-solving processes themselves. Much of the writing that occurs in schools has authentic purposes other than publication. These types of writing are often overshadowed by the emphasis on a formal, process orientation. Writing as a life skill is developed through such activities as

- organizing information
- planning activities
- communicating with peers/adults
- recording personal responses
- recording results of research
- responding to and giving instructions
- questioning
- persuading
- clarifying thinking
- reporting
- writing-in-role; projecting into the experience of another

In all cases, the function of the writing should determine the kind of process it undergoes. Writing is an active, creative process, incorporating at any one time aspects of listening, speaking, reading, viewing, and representing to achieve its goals. Through writing, as with all modes of language, we construct our sense of reality by clarifying, discovering, assessing, reflecting on, resolving, and refining what we truly think and feel about experience. If that writing is meant for a wider, public audience, however, then an effective, efficient, and comprehensive application of revising and editing skills becomes an integral and essential component of the writing.

Too many people, including numerous students, perceive revising and editing as functions grafted on to the writing process; they also have difficulty conceptualizing the two separate, but ultimately linked operations.

What follows is a helpful analogy. Imagine a meal prepared at a four-star restaurant. Since the food is being prepared for public consumption, revision is an intrinsic part of the kitchen's preparations. A client's first expectation is that all matters pertaining to the preparation of the food have been thoroughly and painstakingly examined, both by the chef and the team of sous-chefs. The quality of the food will be uniform; suspect vegetables, for instance, will have been replaced with fresher items or suitable substitutions. The recipes will be tested and well-rehearsed, but invigorated with spontaneous, inventive adjustments, fuelled by experience, talent, and intuition. The substance of the meal is fashioned into a superior and memorable state and ready to be served.

Imagine how that meal will be received, on the other hand, if slapped onto a plate helter-skelter, various sauces misapplied, and discrete items haphazardly mixed together. As is the case with writing, in spite of the deserving nature and quality of the meal itself, the presentation will often determine success or failure. A piece of writing may be thought-provoking and superior in content, but mechanical and usage errors can severely mar its impact. By the same token, the correct and impeccable presentation of a mediocre meal, while pleasing to the eye, disappoints the palate. Slickness of presentation will never disguise shallowness of thought.

Successful writers realize that they are preparing a feast for the mind that will only be fully appreciated if presented in a way that is pleasing to the eye. They first prepare, test, examine, and refine the substance of their thoughts through the revision process. They then meticulously and scrupulously edit the material for pristine presentation. Superior preparation allied with flawless presentation produces both first-class writing or the choicest of meals. An eager audience is hungry for both. When student writers do their part through the revising and editing processes, they can pass the writing on with a hearty *bon appetit!* and be assured that their readers will enjoy a memorable feast.

Glossary

The definitions in this selected glossary reflect the meanings that are used in the text.

Apostrophes (')   These show omissions, possession, or the plural of words that have no plural of their own.

At risk   A descriptor applied to students with academic, emotional, or social difficulties or a combination of these serious enough to jeopardize acceptable progress in school

Brainstorming   Generating a list of examples, ideas, or questions to illustrate, expand, or explore central idea or topic

Camera ready   In a state suitable for publication; a synonym for print ready

Cliché   An expression that has become commonplace and stale through overuse

Collaboration   Problem solving in pairs and in other small groups (see also **co-operative learning**)

Colons (:)   These punctuation marks are used to separate the main part of a sentence from an explanation, example, quotation, or list; also used after the salutation of a business letter, in certain numerical expressions, and between titles and subtitles in books.

Commas (,)   The written equivalents of the pause in everyday speech that break sentences or divide a word series to clarify or prevent ambiguity

Composing   The process of putting words together to form an effective message or artistic statement in speech or writing (not to be confused with **transcribing**)

Conferences   Opportunities to discuss ideas and problems in pairs or in small groups; conferences can be conducted in a variety of formats with and without the teacher.

Co-operative learning   A variety of small-group instructional techniques focusing on peer collaboration

Descriptive essay   A relatively brief literary composition, usually in prose, offering a word picture, rich in details appealing to the senses, of a character, an incident, or a setting

Desktop publishing   Using the resources of the personal computer to give individuals access to the publishing process; software ranges from simple word-processing programs to sophisticated publishing programs offering a variety of text and graphics capabilities

Drafting   The recursive cycle of revising and editing written material

Editing   Checking, prior to a final copy, for errors in spelling, usage, and clarity of expression

Essay   A relatively brief literary composition, usually in prose, giving the author's views on a particular topic

Evaluation   Determining progress towards and attainment of specific goals; assessing student progress and achievement and program effectiveness

Exclamation mark (!)   The punctuation mark used after a word, phrase, or sentence to provide to provide emphasis

Free verse   Unrhyming verse with an irregular metrical pattern and length of line

Fluency   The ability to speak, write, or read aloud smoothly, easily, and with clear expression of ideas

Grammar   A study of the patterns of word formation in a language and the structure of word order in sentences, clauses, and phrases

Haiku   A type of Japanese poem written in seventeen syllables with three lines of five, seven, and five syllables, respectively, to express a single thought or evoke a specific response

Homograph   A word with the same spelling as another word, regardless of pronunciation

Homonym   A word with the same oral or written form as another word. The term *homonym* covers both homophones and homographs.

Homophone   A word with the same pronunciation as another word, regardless of spelling

Hyphens   These marks are used to indicate that part of a word is carried over to the next line, to connect parts of a compound word, or in special circumstances with numbers.

Metacognition   The study of thought processes

Modelling   The act of serving as an example of a behavior: e.g., a teacher reads during independent reading periods, displays a genuine courtesy towards others and a respect for individual differences, or demonstrates revision strategies on a piece of his or her own writing

Optic poetry   Often called concrete poetry; the arrangement of words in some form of graphic representation to reinforce the meaning or theme

Paragraph   One or more sentences about a single topic, grouped together, and usually with an indented first line

Peer editing   With a partner or small group, checking, prior to a final copy, for errors in spelling, usage, and clarity of expression

Period   The sign that signifies the full pause at the end of a declarative sentence. A period can also highlight the use of an abbreviation.

Personal response   Encouraging students to begin an explication of and reflection on material with their own idiosyncratic, immediate, and spontaneous impressions, reactions, and questions where and when they arise; includes the recognition that our listening, speaking, reading, writing, viewing, and thinking processes are directed towards "making meaning"

Poem   A composition in which word images are selected and arranged to create an especially vivid, powerful, or beautiful impression on the listener or reader

Pre-writing (rehearsing)   Activities and experiences occurring before the writing begins; includes talking, reading, and picture making

Project   An extended school assignment, such as a research investigation, a formal experiment, or an elaborate collection

Proofreading   The final editing stage prior to publication

Prose narrative   A form of writing in which a person tells a story, actual or fictional

Punctuation   The use of approved, specific marks other than letters to help clarify the meaning in something written

Question mark (?)   The punctuation mark used at the end of a sentence to indicate that the sentence is a question

Quotation marks (" ")   These are used to indicate the beginning and end of a directly quoted passage or to enclose a word or phrase used in an unusual way.

Read-alouds   Any material read aloud, often by the teacher; can be both fiction and non-fiction

Revision   This process includes substituting, adding, deleting, and reordering words, phrases, sentences, sections, and ideas.

Scribe One who transcribes the words of another

Semicolon (;)   These punctuation marks are used sometimes to separate but still join two independent, but related statements; they also separate items in a series that already contain punctuation.

Sentence   A word or words grouped together to convey meaning, often, but not always, containing two elements: what you are talking about (the subject) and what you want to say about it (the predicate)

Sentence combining   A teaching technique in which students build a single complex sentence from a series of simple sentences

Spell check   The editing feature of word-processing software programs that offers lists of alternatives to questionable spellings

Transcribing   Writing out or typing a copy; the physical act as distinguished from the creative process (see **composing**)

Usage   The customary or preferred way of using specific items of language in such areas as pronunciation, vocabulary, and syntax

Word   As author Frank Smith put it, a sequence of letters with a white space on either side. These small units may contain meaning by themselves or help express meaning in association with other words.

Writer's workshop   Organizing the classroom writing program to reflect and facilitate the writing process; includes such components as regular use of a writing folder; collaboration among students for composing, revising, and editing; and regular student-teacher writing conferences. Frequent sharing and publishing of student writing are often important features.

Writing folder   A folder or notebook organized to accommodate and facilitate the various stages in the writing process

Writing process   The recursive and blended elements of writing: pre-writing, writing, post-writing; includes writing for audiences other than the teacher and for purposes other than summative evaluation

Summary of Reproducible Pages for Students

Checklists/Surveys

Guidelines

Index